SpringerBriefs in Computer S

T0280430

Series Editors
Stan Zdonik
Peng Ning
Shashi Shekhar
Jonathan Katz
Xindong Wu
Lakhmi C. Jain
David Padua
Xuemin Shen
Borko Furht
VS Subrahmanian

For further volumes:
http://www.springer.com/series/10028

Jiming Chen • Jialu Fan • Youxian Sun

Data Dissemination and Query in Mobile Social Networks

 Springer

Jiming Chen
Zhejiang University
Hangzhou, P.R. China
jmchen@ieee.org

Youxian Sun
Zhejiang University
Hangzhou, P.R. China

Jialu Fan
Zhejiang University
Hangzhou, P.R. China

ISSN 2191-5768   ISSN 2191-5776 (electronic)
ISBN 978-1-4614-2253-2   ISBN 978-1-4614-2254-9 (eBook)
DOI 10.1007/978-1-4614-2254-9
Springer New York Heidelberg Dordrecht London

Library of Congress Control Number: 2012935429

Printed on acid-free paper

Springer is part of Springer Science+Business Media (www.springer.com)

Contents

1 Introduction to Mobile Social Networks 1
  1.1 Background and Definition 1
  1.2 Key Features 2
      1.2.1 User Mobility 2
      1.2.2 Opportunistic Networking 2
      1.2.3 Personal Devices 3
  1.3 Potential Applications 4
      1.3.1 Telemedicine for Rural Regions 4
      1.3.2 Social Network Services for the Developing World 4
      1.3.3 Communication under Oppressive Governments 5
      1.3.4 File Sharing and Bulk Data Transfer 6
      1.3.5 Share Air Minutes 6
  1.4 Research Topics and Related Concepts 7
      1.4.1 Realistic Social Contact Traces 7
      1.4.2 User Mobility Model 9
      1.4.3 Routing and Forwarding Techniques 12
      1.4.4 Data Dissemination and Query Schemes 15

2 Data Dissemination in MSNets 19
  2.1 Introduction 19
  2.2 Overview 21
      2.2.1 Two Observations from Realistic MSNet Traces 21
      2.2.2 Big Picture 22
      2.2.3 Optimization Objectives 23
  2.3 Trace-based Analysis on Mobile Social Networks 24
      2.3.1 Experimental Traces 25
      2.3.2 Geographic Regularity of User Mobility 25
      2.3.3 Geo-Community 28
      2.3.4 Geo-Centrality 30
  2.4 User Mobility Model 31
      2.4.1 User's Sojourn Time Distribution over Geo-Communities .. 32

2.4.2   Time Homogeneous Semi-Markov Model............... 33
2.4.3   Steady-state Probability Distribution over geo-Communities   33
2.4.4   Similarity of Users' Steady-State Distributions in Different
        Time-Scales... 36
2.5   Designing Algorithms for the Superuser Route 37
2.5.1   Static Route Algorithm 37
2.5.2   Greedy Adaptive Route Algorithm...................... 40
2.6   Performance Evaluation 42
2.6.1   Simulation Setup 42
2.6.2   Performance Comparison 45
2.6.3   Fairness of a User-Superuser Meeting Among Users 48
2.6.4   Simulation Summary 48
2.7   Discussions 49
2.7.1   Interest-based Data Dissemination 49
2.7.2   Multiple Superuser Scheduling 49
2.7.3   Incentive Scheme in Selfish MSNets 49
2.8   Related Work 50
2.9   Conclusions 51

3   Data Query in MSNets... 53
3.1   Introduction 53
3.2   Preliminaries and Overview 55
3.2.1   Network Models and Assumptions...................... 55
3.2.2   Information Search in DTNs: A Scenario 55
3.2.3   The Basic Idea 56
3.2.4   Trace-based Analysis on Neighbors' Mobility Range 57
3.3   DelQue Scheme 58
3.4   Computing Utilities from Social Patterns and Mobility 60
3.4.1   Transient Behavior of Time-Homogeneous Semi-Markov
        Model.. 60
3.4.2   Spatio-Temporal Prediction of User Mobility 61
3.4.3   Computation of Utilities 63
3.5   Performance Evaluation 64
3.5.1   Simulation Setup 64
3.5.2   Comparison Results 66
3.5.3   Impact of p and λ............................ 66
3.5.4   Performance Comparison between QSS and QMS......... 68
3.5.5   Spatio-Temporal Prediction Evaluation 69
3.6   Related Work 72
3.6.1   Internet Search Engines 72
3.6.2   Decentralized Search Schemes in Unstructured Ad-Hoc
        Networks 73
3.6.3   Information Search Schemes in DTNs 73
3.7   Conclusion 75

4   Conclusions and Future Work 77
4.1   Energy Efficient Sleep Scheduling for MSNet 78
4.2   Realization of TCP 78
4.3   Research on Anycast Service 79
4.4   Effective Use of Contact Duration 79

References 81

Chapter 1
Introduction to Mobile Social Networks

1.1 Background and Definition

Recently, personal hand-held mobile devices (e.g., MP3 players, PDAs, and smart-phones) have become more and more popular. Mobile users carrying such devices can report two different experiences with network services. The experience is normally good in districts where Internet connectivity is available, and the users can access all Internet applications. On the other hand, in between such "Internet connectivity islands", users are unable to transfer any information, even though the party that the user wishes to communicate with is within range of his/her mobile device and has wireless communication capabilities.

The reason is that the current network services always rely on managed infrastructure (e.g. DNS, DHCP, centralized servers). They employ network protocols requiring continuous connectivity between the communicating parties throughout a transmission (e.g. TCP). These constraints cannot be satisfied easily by mobile devices, which motivates a new networking paradigm to offer services for mobile users even when they are not in reach of Internet connectivity islands. *Mobile social network (MSNet)* emerges as the times require, which can enable mobile users with wireless devices to establish network connectivity, and further disseminate, query and share interesting data among themselves in the absence of network infrastructure.

Since users are only connected intermittently in MSNets, user mobility should be exploited to bridge network partitions and to forward data. Currently, existing data route/forward approaches for such intermittently connected networks are commonly "store-carry-and-forward" schemes, which exploit the physical user movements to carry data around the network and overcome path disconnection. Since the source and destination may be far away from each other, the delay for the destination to receive the data from the source may be long. As a matter of fact, MSNet falls under the more general space of Delay Tolerant Network (DTN), and can be viewed as one type of socially-aware DTNs.

DTN explores networking in the presence of challenged networking conditions, such as links which are often disconnected, or are subject to long delays. To date, activities in the DTN community have addressed various communication environments where standard Internet protocols would be hard to use or would provide poor performance, e.g., networking using buses following pre-defined routes [1], interplanetary networking [2], interfacing with sensor networks [3], and employing mobile nodes to bridge data between remote village networks and the Internet [4] [5].

There is a large quantity of untapped resource in portable devices including local wireless bandwidth (e.g. 802.11 and Bluetooth), storage capacity, and CPU power. The only scarce resource is power, but advances in power engineering and battery technologies have reported that mobile phones can last for one week on a single charge. We envision a world where these resources can be used to provide ad-hoc networking functionality alongside access Internet, and user applications make use of both types of bandwidth transparently. This is the goal of Mobile Social Networks.

1.2 Key Features

We now discuss some key features of the MSNets space.

1.2.1 User Mobility

Mobility is a double-edged sword. Since quantities of data can be carried across the network, user mobility has the potential to increase network bandwidth. On the other hand, mobility also makes it challenging to communicate with users, as forwarding paths may be unstable and communication among devices may be highly variable.

In MSNets, devices are usually carried by people, so the movement of such devices is strongly influenced by human decisions and social behavior [6], and the social network theory can be employed to analyze the regularities of user mobility in MSNets.

1.2.2 Opportunistic Networking

Internet routing assumes there exists a contemporaneous path between two nodes. The Mobile Ad-hoc Network (MANET) community focuses on techniques for determining end-to-end paths in a mobile network However, MSNet does not aim to build end-to-end paths, but takes advantage of any opportunity in the process of user mobility to forward data hop-by-hop. One type of opportunity is found in local network connectivity (using wireless or other means). Whenever two mobile users come into contact, they detect each other and determine what to transfer.

In addition to forwarding data using local connection opportunities, an MSNet node may, at some times and in some places, have global connectivity, e.g. via WiFi access infrastructure or GPRS. Note that it is not always the case that global connectivity is more useful than local connectivity. Local networking can provide better service than Internet access if the corresponding party is nearby, either because the correspondent does not themselves have global connectivity, because the traffic requires a high bandwidth or low latency, or because global connectivity is expensive (e.g. in an airport lobby).

On the other hand, for traffic with no local destination, forwarding it towards the Internet (either using global connectivity yourself or by forwarding locally towards nodes with global connectivity) may be the fastest method of reaching the recipient. The tricky part may be in the return path: how does a node on the Internet forward messages to a mobile node which does not itself attach to the Internet, but which passes near other nodes can forward. This is an open problem.

Using both local and global opportunities allows MSNet to provide robust networking for users, as it can transparently switch between local connectivity and global connectivity, especially when the latter is unexpectedly lost. This all-too-often situation can be brought on by hardware failure or software bugs. It may also be useful in situations of disasters, in which users' mobile phones and laptops become useless for communications purposes, but opportunistic networking would allow people to transfer important messages with physical movement.

1.2.3 Personal Devices

Mobile social network targets devices, which remain always-on and are always-held by users. Such devices include mobile phones, PDAs, active RFID tags, and laptops. This implies that personal devices have networking requirements. User-facing applications such as web browsers and email clients must be able to communicate the status of the network (e.g. expected performance for a large number of file transfer) and of individual transactions (e.g. whether an instant message was received).

The primary goal of networking conducted by personal device must be the support of its owner's tasks. Providing networking support for others (e.g. by storing and forwarding data for them) is possible when there is spare resource (CPU, storage, transmission bandwidth, and battery). The maintenance of trust relationships and the provision of incentives may be of important considerations, since selfish behavior would inherently cause node to decline service to others. Security and privacy must also be detected, since data may traverse many uncontrolled and potentially malicious nodes. These are more open issues in the design of MSNet.

1.3 Potential Applications

DTNs have mostly focused on applications such as alleviating the connectivity problems in rural and developing regions, interplanetary and military communication, and other adversary environments where end-to-end connectivity is not feasible. In this section we envision a few potential applications that we believe could have a real impact on the MSNet community.

1.3.1 Telemedicine for Rural Regions

The deployment of telemedicine systems in developing regions is one of the potential services that MSNet can offer. These are areas that are often plagued by diseases that are preventable or curable, if treated properly, but frequently end up killing the person suffering from it. There are several barriers to introducing Information Communication Technology (ICT) solutions in this domain, including high cost, unreliable infrastructure and lack of computer skills among staff [7]. While some telephone systems may exist, nothing that is advanced enough to transmit pictures and other information that can help a doctor diagnose a patient is available. Participatory design sessions with health staff, and pilot studies at clinics in South Africa, suggest that one way to deal with the challenges above is to implement telemedicine using store-carry-and-forward Voice-over-IP (VoIP) [8]. VoIP is accessible from devices that are similar to traditional telephones, and thus can be used by people with little computer skills. VoIP services can also be developed relatively cheaper because of the availability of open source software, and can be deployed without fixed infrastructure or support from a network operator [9]. The store-carry-and-forward nature of such a service makes it ideal for deployment over an MSNet. Even though a purely voice-based system is fairly simple and will only help with minor diagnostics, once a system like that is in place, it is easy to deploy new services that include images and other media to improve the possibility for doctors to give the correct diagnose and prescribe treatment.

1.3.2 Social Network Services for the Developing World

The lack of Internet connectivity in certain regions in no way implies that there is also no need for Social Network Services (SNS). We argue the opposite. Traditionally over the past several thousands of years, when no ICT was available, people have been using local face-to-face communication with their peers to explore their social networks in order to find and exchange information and goods. Because of technology constraints, people in these regions still rely on traditional social networks to distribute information. It is thought that DTN-enabled social network services would be very beneficial to them [10].

The Short Message Service (SMS) available in cellular networks is a communication channel that has seen a rapid growth lately, with 25 billions SMS being sent in India in 2006. This should be compared to 12 billions in 2005, so it is clear that the growth is very rapid [11]. As this has proven to be a true killer app for the cellular networks, we envision that the SNS should try to mimic the simplicity and style of SMS messaging, but offering richer services at a lower cost and even where there is no cellular coverage.

Given the evidence above, and the constraint on network conditions, it could be seen that this type of SNS networking as a potential killer app for opportunistic communication. In addition to typical SNS services such as friend searching and management, the system should offer support for resource sharing, information seeking, and information dissemination. For example, a farmer can send a message via his Bluetooth phone to his friends nearby to advertise the availability of his tomatoes to sell, and the friends can help to propagate the message through the social network.

1.3.3 Communication under Oppressive Governments

Traditionally, the Internet has provided a relative freedom to people to communicate with anyone about any topic. As Internet and related services have become more prevalent in the entire world, this new possibility for communication without control have made it immensely popular among people in locations where governments and other organizations try to control the population in an oppressive way. This was obviously not looked keenly upon by the governments in those countries, and there have been many occurrences of late where censorship, traffic monitoring, and other mechanisms have been put in place to prevent free communication.

Opportunistic communication can become a champion of free speech in such countries. By not using the infrastructure to transmit messages, but only relying on opportunistic forwarding between people, it will become much more difficult for government agencies to track the communication. This is similar to mobile versions of the Tor [12] and Crowds [13] anonymous networks on MSNet, but using mobility and delay of transmission to further increase anonymity.

To make this a reality, much work on security in opportunistic networks must be done. It is important that it is difficult to determine both the original sender of a message and the identities of intermediate forwarders for their safety. It is also vital that a reliable and authenticated method is available to know when a message has been delivered to its destination to avoid rogue agents injecting fake acknowledgements to purge messages from the network.

1.3.4 File Sharing and Bulk Data Transfer

Even in situations where cellular data access is relatively cheap and reliable, the bandwidth offered by such services tends to be orders of magnitude smaller than what is offered by home broadband networks and also local wireless communication technologies. Thus, it is not very appealing to use the cellular data network to transfer large files. It is often better to only use the cellular network to transmit the request for some content, and then use delay tolerant techniques to deliver the data to the mobile device. While this technique can improve performance for dissemination of all types of large data items, it is even more beneficial if the data access patterns are somehow localized such that users in a certain area are more likely to request a certain data item (could be a video of the local news, or the course work among a group of students). Such properties increase the probability that data can be found locally among other nodes, and as such improve performance.

In large cities, where people meet many others every day, for example in public transportation systems, it is likely that the network of opportunistic contacts will be dense enough to provide a good means of spreading information, especially information that is likely to be of interest to a large part of the population such as the latest newscast or a new episode of a popular TV series (which of course creates a whole new set of challenges regarding copyright and DRM issues that will have to be addressed as part of designing this system).

In addition to purely opportunistic forwarding between mobile nodes, network operators can add storage to the network such that if it is possible to predict where nodes are moving, parts of the content can be prefetched to WiFi hotspots where the user will pass in the future for fast download [14]. This can also be combined with the opportunistic forwarding between nodes as it has been shown that utilizing a combination of opportunistic forwarding and access points can greatly improve performance of such content dissemination in networks of sparse infrastructure [15].

There are several benefits for the operators to add such services to their networks. First of all, they gain a new service that they can offer their customers for added value. In addition, this method of content distribution can also reduce the operating expenses for the operator. If users are already paying a flat rate for data access, there is no added benefit for the operator when users download more content, but instead it will only consume network resources. Utilizing opportunistic communication will enable them to offer the same service, but with less resource usage. Operators have already realized this issue on fixed network, and tried to use MSNet-like approaches to do bulk data transfer on the Internet [16]. We believe this will sooner or later happen to the cellular network if a flat rate is imposed on the service.

1.3.5 Share Air Minutes

Even with ubiquitous availability of 3G coverage with a low flat rate for data traffic and excess air minutes for voice traffic, many mobile phone users are still on a pay-as-you-go mode, where pre-paid credits are bought and used for calls. In addition, users located outside the coverage area of their own operator pay excessive roaming charges to use the network of another operator. It is possible to leverage opportunistic networking in such a scenario by allowing the contract users to share their excess air minutes to the prepaid card users, or from the local contract users to the roaming users.

Hui et al. proposed using opportunistic networking to allow mobile phone users to share their unused contract minutes [17]. A prepaid card/roaming user can connect her phone to a sharer's phone and make her own phone act as a headset of the sharer. The shared phone acting as the server then diverts the voice traffic to the cellular network via the phone's cellular link. There is a well defined business model here: the contract user would benefit from selling their unused minutes, the pre-pay users would benefit from cheaper calls, and the operators can gain extra revenue on minutes that have already been sold if they could receive a percentage of the value of the resold minutes.

While this is technically possible today, in order to realize such a system, a system must be developed where phones are able to estimate if there are excess minutes available or if the contract user will need them all himself/herself. This could initially be manually configured, but should ideally be automated. A major challenge (which could also enable other applications) is how to deal with the micro-payments of air time in a secure manner. In order to be able to maintain calls of acceptable length, it is also important to be able to estimate which person will remain in range of local wireless communication long enough to finish the phone call.

1.4 Research Topics and Related Concepts

Thanks to the new communication paradigm where communication is possible even if end-to-end connectivity is never achievable, MSNets have attracted a lot of attentions from the wireless and mobile network research community. In just a few years, the research area has gone from a small topic considered fairly obscure by most researchers, to a topic that is very hot. It can be found more and more new conferences, workshops, and journals dedicated to the field start appearing. A large amount of work has been done on collecting realistic social contact traces, studying user mobility models, developing routing and forwarding techniques, and exploring data dissemination and query schemes.

1.4.1 Realistic Social Contact Traces

To study the properties of contacts between people, there are several recent public data repository of traces capturing movement of human-carried mobile devices. Examples are GPS traces and Bluetooth connectivity traces (i.e., traces containing the

Table 1.1 Trace Studied

Trace	UCSD	Vehicular	MITcell	MITbt	Cambridge	Infocom
Network type	WiFi	GPS	GSM	Bluetooth	Bluetooth	Bluetooth
Duration	77 days	6 months	16 months	16 months	11.5 days	3 days
No. of devices	275	196	89	89	36	41
Contacts	116,383	9,588	891,891,024	114,046	21,203	28,216
Mean Inter-contact Time	24 hours	20.8 hours	3.5 hours	87 hours	14 hours	3.3 hours
Year	2002	2004	2004	2004	2005	2005

Bluetooth identifiers of the devices that have been in radio range of a device). For instance, researchers at the Intel Research Laboratory and the University of Cambridge distributed Bluetooth devices to people, in order to collect data about human movements and study the characteristics of the colocation patterns among people. These experiments were firstly conducted among students and researchers in Cambridge [18] and then among the participants of INFOCOM 2005, 2006 [19]. Examples of similar projects are the Wireless Topology Discovery project at UCSD [20] and the campus-wide WiFi traffic measurements that have been carried out at Dartmouth College [21]. At this institution, a project with the aim of creating a repository of publicly available traces for the mobile networking community has also been started [22].

Table 1.1 summarizes the diverse characteristics of several public traces in terms of their duration, wireless technology used and environment of collection. the datasets can be grouped in three distinct types:

- *Infrastructure-based* traces that reflect connectivity between existing infrastructure, e.g., Access Points (APs) or cells, and wireless mobile devices (UCSD [20] & MITcell [23] datasets in Table 1.1). These datasets describe association times of a specific mobile device with an AP or cell.
- *Direct contact* traces that record contacts directly between mobile devices (e.g., imotes) and were collected by distributing devices to a number of people, usually students or conference attendees (Cambridge [24], Infocom & MITbt datasets in Table 1.1). These datasets describe start and end contact times for each pair of mobile devices.
- *GPS-based* contacts through a private trace collected by tracking the movements of individual people of a large corporation through GPS units. The GPS units were placed in volunteers cars for approximately four months and overall the trace covers the metropolitan area of a large US city (Vehicular dataset [25] in Table 1.1). The dataset logs the latitude and longitude coordinates of each mobile device every approximately 10 seconds.

1.4.2 User Mobility Model

Mobility models are used to simulate and evaluate the performance of mobile wireless systems and the algorithms and protocols at the basis of them. The definition of realistic mobility models is one of the most critical and, at the same time, difficult aspects of the simulation of applications and systems designed for mobile environments. There are essentially two possible types of mobility patterns that can be used to evaluate mobile network protocols and algorithms by means of simulations: traces and synthetic models [26]. Traces are obtained by means of measurements of deployed systems and usually consist of logs of connectivity or location information, whereas synthetic models are mathematical models, such as sets of equations, which try to capture the movement of the devices.

1.4.2.1 Purely Synthetic Models

The simplest mobility model is the Random Walk mobility model [27] [28], also called Brownian motion; it is a widely used model to represent purely random movements of the entities of a system in various disciplines from physics to meteorology. However, it cannot be considered as a suitable model to simulate wireless environments, since human movements do not present the continuous changes of direction that characterize this mobility model.

Another example of random mobility model is the Random Way-Point mobility model [29]. This can be considered as an extension of the Random Walk mobility model, with the addition of pauses between changes in direction or speed. However, also in this case, the realism of the model in terms of geographical movement is far from being realistic.

In [30] [31], the authors presented a generalization of the Random Walk and Random Way-Point mobility models that they call Random Trip model. The authors introduced a technique to sample the initial simulation state from the stationary regime (a methodology that is usually called perfect simulation) based on Palm Calculus [32] in order to solve the problem of reaching time-stationarity. Perfect simulation for the Random Way-Point model was originally proposed by Navidi and Camp in [33].

1.4.2.2 Trace-based Mobility Models

In recent years, many researchers have tried to refine existing models in order to make them more realistic by exploiting the available mobility traces [22]. The key underlying idea of these models is the exploitation of available measurements such as connectivity logs to generate synthetic traces that are characterized by the same statistical properties of the real ones.

Various pioneering measurement studies have been conducted both in infrastructure-based and infrastructure-less environments since the first wireless networks have been deployed. Extensive measurements about the usage of the early deployed Wireless Local Area Networks (WLANs) have been conducted, for instance, in [34], in [35], and in [36]. A detailed analysis of the usage of the WLAN of the Dartmouth College campus is presented in [21].

The first examples of mobility models are based on traces of WLAN campus usage. In [37] a mobility model based on real data from the campus WLAN at ETH in Zurich is presented. The authors used a simulation area divided into squares and derive the probability of transitions between adjacent squares from the data of the access points. Also in this case, the session duration data follow a power-law distribution. This approach can be considered as a refined version of the Weighted Way-Point mobility model [38] [39]. The authors of this model represented the probability of user movements between different areas of the USC campus by means of a Markov model. The model is extracted from data collected from user surveys (i.e., the users were asked to keep a diary of their movements for one month).

The Model T and its evolution, the Model T++, proposed in [40] and [41] generate traces also mirroring the spatial registration patterns of user movements inside a campus WLAN (i.e., the connections to the access points spread in the campus area). The authors defined the concept of popularity gradient between different access points and its influence on user movements. This model was evaluated using traces from Dartmouth College. In [42], another model extracted from real traces based on the study of probability of transitions between different locations was presented. The evaluation of the model was essentially based on the matching of the geographical movements and density of users, rather than on the analysis of the patterns of connectivity among them.

A mobility model based on the extraction of user mobility characteristics from the wireless network traces of the Dartmouth College WLAN was presented in [43]. The authors defined popular regions in the campus and characterize the transitions among these areas by means of a Markovian model. Another key finding of the authors was the fact that pause time and speed follow log-normal distributions. These models only represented the transitions between five and six locations respectively. The data presented characteristics, similar to [43], that evidently differed from those generated by means of classic synthetic random mobility models. In [44], Resta and Santi presented a model of user movement between access points driven by the quality of service perceived by the users themselves. This approach is very generic and it is composed of different models that allow for the simulation of user mobility, network traffic, underlying wireless technology and quality of service.

Another interesting model representing the movement inside downtown Osaka was discussed in [45]: the authors reproduced the movements of pedestrians by analyzing the characteristics of the crowd in subsequent instants of time and maps of the city using an empirical methodology, without relying on any wireless measurements.

With respect to mobility models for vehicular networks, a large amount of traces mapping the movements of vehicles in cities and in highways are collected by the traffic authorities but they are not publicly available also for security reasons. Starting from these traces and from empirical observations, several models have been recently presented. Examples include the model proposed by Saha and Johnson [46] extracted from the TIGER traces, GrooveSim [47] and STRAW [48].

Finally, a model for the generation of the inter-contacts time duration between buses derived from the log traces of the DieselNet was presented in [49]. It should be noted that this was not a mobility model, but a connectivity model, i.e., it was used to represent topological but not geographical information over time.

1.4.2.3 Community-based Mobility Models

In this subsection, recent developments of mobility modeling [6] are discussed, i.e., the introduction of social networking concepts as a basis of the representation of people movements. These models are usually trace based, i.e., they are generally founded or evaluated by means of real traces. The modeling of these relationships and their implications to human mobility is of paramount importance to test protocols and systems that exploit the underlying social structure, such as socially-aware delay tolerant forwarding protocols [50] [51].

Social network mobility models are based on a simple observation. In mobile networks, devices are usually carried by humans, so the movement of such devices is necessarily based on human decisions and social behavior. A key characteristic is the presence of clusters that are usually dependent on the relationships among the members of the social group. In order to capture this type of behavior, mobility models dependent on the structure of the relationships among people carrying the devices have been defined. However, existing group mobility models fail to capture this social dimension [26].

In [52], the authors proposed the community based mobility model, founded on social network theory. A key input of the mobility model is the social network that links the individuals carrying the mobile devices in order to generate realistic synthetic network structures [53]. The model allows collections of hosts to be grouped together in a way that is based on social relationships among the individuals. This grouping is only then mapped to a topographical space, with topography biased by the strength of social ties. The movements of the hosts are also driven by the social relationships among them. The model also allows for the definition of different types of relationships during a certain period of time (i.e., a day or a week). For instance, it might be important to be able to describe that in the morning and in the afternoon of weekdays, relationships at the workplace are more important than friendships and family one, whereas the opposite is true during the evenings and weekends.

Another notable example of mobility model founded on the social relationships between the individuals carrying the mobile devices was presented in [28]. This work is based on assumptions similar to [52], but it is considerably more limited in scope. Hosts are statically assigned to a particular group during the initial configuration process, whereas [52] accounts for movement between groups. Moreover, the authors claimed that MANETs were scale-free, but the typical properties of scale-free networks were not considered in the design of the model presented by the authors. The scale-free distribution of mobile ad hoc networks is still not proven in general, since very limited measurements are available and it is worth noting that the scale-free properties are strictly dependent on the movements of hosts and, therefore, they are dependent on the actual application scenarios [54]. The idea of using communities to represent group movements in an infrastructured WiFi network has also been exploited in [55] and in its time-variant extension presented in [56]. More specifically, this model preserves two fundamental characteristics, the skewed location visiting preferences and the periodical re-appearance of nodes in the same location. Recently, Ekman et al. proposed a model based on the daily activities of the users (and group of users) and their movements between place of interests in a city map [57].

1.4.3 Routing and Forwarding Techniques

In this subsection, a number of important issues in any routing algorithm are considered: the routing objective, the amount of knowledge about the network required by the scheme, when routes are computed, the use of multiple paths, and the use of source routing. We focus on how these issues arise in the context of MSNet routing problem. The routing objective of traditional routing schemes has been to select a path which minimizes some simple metric (e.g. the number of hops). For MSNets, however, the most desirable objective is not immediately obvious.

One natural objective is to maximize the probability of message delivery. Messages could potentially be lost due to creation of a routing loop or the forced discarding of data when buffers are exhausted. As an approximation, we focus on minimizing the delay of a message (the time between when it is injected and when it is completely received).

While MSNet applications are expected to be tolerant of delay, this does not mean that they would not benefit from decreased delay. Furthermore, it is believed this metric is an appropriate measure to use in exploring the differential evaluation of several routing algorithms in an application-independent manner. Minimizing delay lowers the time messages spend in the network, reducing contention for resources (in a qualitative sense). Therefore, lowering delay indirectly improves the probability of message delivery. This is validated by our simulation results.

1.4.3.1 Proactive Routing vs. Reactive Routing

In proactive routing, routes are computed automatically and independently of traffic arrivals. Most Internet standard routing protocols and some ad-hoc protocols such as DSDV (Destination Sequenced Distance Vector) and OLSR (Optimized Link-State Routing) are examples of this style [58]. In an MSNet, these protocols are capable of computing routes for a connected subgraph of the overall MSNet topology graph. They fail when asked to provide paths to nodes which are not currently reachable. Despite this drawback, proactive network-layer routing protocols may provide useful input to MSNet routing algorithm by providing the set of currently-reachable nodes from which MSNet routing may select preferred next hops.

In reactive routing, routes are discovered on-demand when traffic must be delivered to an unknown destination. Ad-hoc routing protocols such as AODV (Ad-hoc On-demand Distance Vector) and DSR (Dynamic Source Routing) are examples of this style [58]. In these systems, a route discovery protocol is employed to determine routes to destinations on-demand, incurring additional delay. These protocols work best when communication patterns are relatively sparse. For an MSNet, as with the proactive protocols, these protocols work only for finding routes in a connected subgraph of the overall MSNet routing graph. However, they fail in a different way than the proactive protocols. In particular, they will simply fail to return a successful route (from a lack of response), whereas the proactive protocols can potentially fail more quickly (by determining that the requested destination is not presently reachable).

In an MSNet, routes may vary with time in predictable ways and can be pre-computed using knowledge about future topology dynamics. Employing a proactive approach would likely involve computing several sets of routes and indexing them by time. The associated resource requirements would be prohibitive unless the traffic demand is large and a large percentage of the possible network nodes exchange traffic. Otherwise, a reactive approach would be more attractive.

A related issue is *route stability*, a measure of how long the currently-known routes are valid. Route stability depends on the rate of topological change. With relatively stable routes one can employ route caching to avoid unnecessary routing protocol exchanges. With future knowledge about topology changes, caching could be especially effective in an MSNet because it may be possible to know ahead of time exactly when to evict existing cached route entries.

1.4.3.2 Source Routing vs Per-hop Routing

In source routing the complete path of a message is determined at the source node, and encoded in some way in the message. The route is therefore determined once and does not change as the message traverses the network. In contrast, in per-hop routing the next-hop of a message is determined at each hop along its forwarding path. Per-hop routing allows a message to utilize local information about available contacts and queues at each hop, which is typically unavailable at the source. Thus, per-hop routing may lead to better performance. Unfortunately, due to its local nature, it may lead to loops when nodes have different topological views (e.g. due to incomplete or delayed routing information).

1.4.3.3 Message Splitting

A message is split when forwarded in such a way that different parts (fragments) are routed along different paths (or across different contacts on the same path). This technique may reduce the delay or improve load balancing among multiple links. It is particularly relevant in MSNets because messages can be arbitrarily large and may not fit in a single contact. However, splitting complicates routing because, in addition to determining the sizes of the fragments, we also have to determine corresponding paths for the fragments.

1.4.3.4 Using Social Context

Another hot research topic is exploiting the social context of users for data forwarding. Su et al. [59] described an experiment in a campus environment to test the feasibility of using mobility and opportunistic pair-wise contact, to form an ad hoc network. They did not use any predetermined mobility model. They concluded that the user mobility can be used to form a network. The Haggle project introduced in 2006 connects humans with mobile devices, in an MSNet fashion. Humans carry mobile devices with them. These devices have processing and storage capacity which can be utilized for data transmission in an MSNet environment.

Spyropoulos et al. [55] stated that the assumptions made in traditional mobility models do not hold in real-life situations. They proposed a heterogeneous community based mobility model, that captures real-life mobility features. They claimed that their model is highly tunable and analytically tractable. Miklas et al. [60] relied on this concept and established that separating people into two groups of friends and strangers, results in a more efficient routing protocol. It also provides more effective security management and higher query hit rate in mobile applications. The authors also showed that human encounter has diurnal and weekly cycles. Simulations proved that social information provides substantial performance improvement. In a similar work done by Yoneki et al. [61], four categories of nodes were proposed: familiar, familiar stranger, stranger and friend. This is an improvement over [60].

Srinivasan et al. [62] studied and characterized mobility patterns in a campus of 22341 students. The daily class schedule was used to infer their contact pattern. They demonstrated that contact patterns can be exploited to design efficient aggregation algorithms. Using the contact data, they also designed aggregation algorithms, in which with a small number of nodes, a large fraction of the data was aggregated. Chaintreau et al. [24] also studied how human mobility can be utilized in opportunistic forwarding. They modelled the distribution of contact times and inter contact times between nodes, using the observed real traces and found that it follows power-law distributions with heavy tail. They also found that models like Random Waypoint and Random Walk do not model heavy tails and so are not the best choices to study realistic opportunistic networks. Musolesi et al. [52] built on this and proposed Community based Mobility Models (CMM). They showed that CMM has the heavy tail characteristics for contact and inter-contact times. They also showed that MANET protocols worked better when CMM model was used. Ekman et al. [57] presented another mobility model that closely follows the everyday life of an average person.

Boldrini et al. [63] continued on the work of Chaintreau et al. [24] and Musolesi et al. [52] to understand how the mobility pattern of users affect the performance of routing protocols. They based their study on group mobility models. They studied how different human mobility patterns impact on the routing performance in opportunistic network. In this work, they concluded that context (social information) based routing schemes reduce congestion and provide acceptable QoS with much lower overhead.

Boldrini et al. [64] used the history of the social relationships among users as the context. Each node maintains its own Identity Table (IT) and that of its neighbours. The proposed algorithm is named HiBOp, and it is able to automatically learn the connectivity opportunities determined by the users movement patterns and exploit them efficiently.

The work of Daly et al. [50] introduced a new metric called betweenness, to forward data. Betweenness is one of the ways to measure the centrality of a node. Centrality of node is an expression of its relative importance in the network. In a social network, it indicates how important a person is. It is also a measure of the extent to which a person (node) has control over the information flowing between two other nodes. Routing decisions can be based on betweenness. In this case, all decisions are made solely on local calculations. Hui et al. [65] proposed the bubble algorithm, which is also based on the two aspects of a society, viz. community and centrality. The bubble algorithm identifies the popular nodes in the source community and the destination community. They play an important role in message transfer. Boldrini et al. [66] also proposed a data dissemination system, which is based on the social relationship between users.

The work of Yoneki et al. [67] on this theme introduced the idea of correlated interaction. They identify social communities and hubs within communities. An overlay network is then built between these hubs. Their work also included three community detection algorithms.

Another work in [68] also exploited the social relationship to transmit messages. Here they proposed the ContentPlace framework. When a node makes contact with another, it advertises the data objects it is interested in and also exchanges summaries of the data objects it carries. Utility value is attached to each data object. This enables the nodes to decide where to place a data object, so that its availability can be optimized. Continuing in this line, the authors of Ioannidis et al. [69] studied how the social network can assist in distribution of dynamic content.

1.4.4 Data Dissemination and Query Schemes

There have been several theoretical and empirical works on how social behavior can be used to improve the performance of data access in delay tolerant networks. PeopleNet [70] is a wireless virtual social network which mimics the way people seek information via social networking. It is simple and scalable for efficient information search in a distributed manner. However, it uses infrastructure to propagate data and queries, which is different from the peer-to-peer MANET scenario. Sim-Bet Routing [50] studied the "small-world" phenomenon of human society and used ego-centric centrality and its social similarity to guide data forwarding. Messages are forwarded towards the node with higher centrality. Similarly, BUBBLE Rap [65] focused on community and social centrality,and nodes are structured into communities. High popularity nodes and community members of the destination are selected as relays. Ghosh et al. [71] have identified the orbital movement pattern of human being and relay nodes are chosen based on the places that they frequently visit. Similarly, Costa et al. [51] provided a routing framework using social interaction information in publish-subscribe systems and Gao et al. [72] study the social-aware multicasting issues in delay tolerant networks. Bai and Helmy [73] studied the last encounter based routing protocol that utilized encounter history to create time gradients for information diffusion in wireless networks. Furthermore, Gao and Cao [74] exploited transient contact patterns to improve the performance of data forwarding, and Li et al. [75] considered the selfishness property of social nodes in data forwarding. Although [75] [76] have applied sociological knowledge to data dissemination in MSNets, these works considered the problem of diffuse data to one pre-determined destination node. Unlike these existing works, data dissemination is not for settings with a specific destination.

The aforementioned works aim to find the most suitable relay node to increase the possibility of reaching the final destination. Miklas et al. [60], Karagiannis et al. [77], Chaintreau et al. [24] and Wang et al. [78] studied the social factor of delay tolerant networks in different ways. They analyzed the distribution of inter-contact time between mobile devices and concluded that the inter-contact time followed the power law distribution or the exponential decay distribution. Further, Hsu et al. [79] analyzed wireless users behavioral patterns by extensively mining wireless network logs and discovered that the size of distinct WLAN user group followed a power-law distribution. Besides, in the area of vehicular MSNets, algorithms [80] and [81] have been proposed for finding the right relays for data forwarding and Kapadia et al. [82] considered the problem of optimizing the replication profile of content to minimize the aggregate average data access delay given knowledge of content popularity. In [83], the authors also presented a cache replacement policy for finite buffers in a vehicular network that takes into account the differing interests of vehicles in different geographic locations, but this work did not explicitly consider social interactions between users. Our work differs from these works in that we study how to use the social network results to improve data dissemination through social aware data diffusion schemes.

Data dissemination can be modeled as spreading of infectious disease. Disease spreading in fixed networks has been studied in the past [84]. [85] also analyzed the epidemic spreading in mobile networks. Different from the analysis in [84] and [85] where all nodes have the same moving and interest features, in our data diffusion scenario, both the interested nodes and uninterested nodes can help diffuse data and they have different meeting frequency and different interest preference. Therefore, different infection and immunization rates between interested and uninterested nodes are studied and the overall diffusion rates by both interested and uninterested nodes are investigated in our work, which adds complexity to the analysis.

Chapter 2
Data Dissemination in MSNets

2.1 Introduction

Mobile Social Networks are networks in which mobile social users physically interact with each other and further reach network service, even in the absence of network infrastructure or end-to-end connectivity [69] [86]. MSNets can be viewed as a kind of socially-aware Delay/Disruption Tolerant Networks (DTNs). Thanks to the popularization of smartphones (e.g., iPhone, Nokia N95, and Blackberry), MSNets have begun to attract more attention to be deployed in a number of critical areas, including large-scale disaster recovery, battlefields, vehicular ad hoc networks, and wide-area sensor networks. However, the intermittent and uncertain network connectivity makes data dissemination in MSNets a challenging problem.

Broadcasting is the operation of sending data from a source user to all other users in the network, which is frequently used in many applications of mobile ad hoc networks (MANETs) [87] [88]. On the other hand, the existing work in intermittently connected networks always focuses on data unicast [65] [89] or multicast [72]. However, broadcast is more effective for data dissemination in such opportunistic environments. Most of the envisioned services (ranging from safety applications to traffic management [90]) rely on broadcasting data to the users inside a certain area of interest. For example, location-based services (product prices, tourist points of interest, etc.) can be advertised from salesmen to the near-by users.

In this chapter, we focus on data broadcasting from a single special user to all other users in MSNets. Specifically, the special mobile user is called *superuser*, and the other regular users are called *users* for short. With the knowledge of users' movements, data broadcasting depends mainly on the mobility trajectory of the superuser. Therefore, the design of a superuser route has a significant impact on network performance. Although there is some similar work on special user route design, such as Message Ferry [91] [92] or Data MULEs [93], they always assume that the special users move with fixed routes [91] to facilitate connectivity among other users, or aim to deal with energy conservation rather than data transmission [93]. The ferry trajectory in SCFR [94] is semi-deterministic depending on the traffic rate. However, it

19

considers the network with static nodes. Tariq et al. [95] proposed a customized ferry route for mobile networks, but the node mobility is strongly constrained. Besides, none of them considers the characteristics of user mobility in realistic MSNets.

Our primary goal is to design flexible superuser routes for data broadcasting in MSNets, without any constraint on the movements of regular users. Hence, the main challenge is how to characterize and represent user mobility in MSNets. From a social network perspective, people sharing interesting properties (e.g., common hobbies, social functions, and occupations) tend to form a *community*. Through trace-based study, we detect an interesting phenomenon: *community always strongly relates to geography in MSNets*. For example, graduate students working in the same office form a community, and they always contact each other in the office. Therefore, *geo-community* is proposed, which represents a geography-related community, into MSNets as a fundamental structure. By means of geo-community, we characterize user mobility and further design superuser route to actively broadcast data to mobile social users in the network.

The works in this chapter are as follows:

- Three datasets are used, which are collected from realistic MSNet environments, to study the characteristics of user mobility. The experiment results show that people in a human society also express geographic regularity, as a supplementary of social attribute. Therefore, *geo-community* is proposed into MSNets to characterize both geographic and social regularities of user mobility.
- Through trace-based study, it is shown that the sojourn time during which a user is associated with a geo-community does not follow the exponential, but instead a power-law distribution. Hence, user mobility over geo-communities in MSNets is formulated as semi-Markov model.
- With the aid of semi-Markov model, each user's steady-state probability distribution over geo-communities can be computed, and *geo-centrality* is further proposed to measure the dynamic user density of each geo-community.
- Considering geo-centrality, *Static Route Algorithms (SRA)* is proposed from a statistic perspective to the superuser that wants to either minimize total duration of the route (*min-T-SRA*) or maximize dessemination ratio (*max-p-SRA*). Furthermore, a *Greedy Adaptive Route Algorithm (GARA)* also is proposed excluding the overlap of contact user sets among the geo-communities.

The remainder of this chapter is organized as follows: Section 2.2 provides an overview of two trace-based observations in MSNets, as well as the big picture and the optimization objectives of our data broadcast scheme. Then, we explore both social and geographic regularities of user mobility in realistic traces, and further propose the concepts of geo-community and geo-centrality into MSNet analysis. Based on such two properties, we employ a semi-Markov process to model user mobility in Section 2.4, and propose superuser route schemes in Section 2.5. Section 2.6 evaluates the performance of our approach via realistic trace-driven simulation. The last three sections present discussions, related work, and conclusions, respectively.

2.2 Overview

In this section, we first introduce two trace-based observations from practical MSNet environments to motivate our proposed broadcast scheme. Then, we give a big picture of the scheme, i.e., the superuser route design problem, whose optimization objectives are finally presented.

2.2.1 Two Observations from Realistic MSNet Traces

Through trace-based study, we have the following two observations:

- *Mobile users in MSNets usually move around several well-visited locations instead of moving randomly.* We explore the realistic traces aiming to reveal the real situation behind such observation. The well-known "small world" phenomenon [96] shows that people usually belong to several communities, and contact others with similar hobbies, occupations, or social functions. For example, graduate students working in the same office interact more frequently with each other. Based on community concept, we further detect that such contact preference is also usually correlated to geography information, such that the contacts among officemates mostly happen in the office. We define such a geography-related community as a *geo-community*, which will be experimentally explored in Section 2.3.3. Furthermore, the user's sojourn time at each geo-community is fairly regular, because their social behavior patterns usually remain stable in a relatively long interval [97].
- *Spatial user distributions are very heterogeneous and possess several geo-communities of high user density.* Since geo-community affiliations among mobile users can be highly diverse, MSNets have some geo-communities of higher user density, and where the superuser therefore has a much better chance of encountering regular users than elsewhere. Examples of such geo-communities include public transportation and shopping centers in urban environments, conference rooms and cafeterias in office buildings, or bases and camps in the military [98], etc. Therefore, we also propose *geo-centrality*, a geography-related centrality metric, into MSNets to measure the user density of geo-communities. Such a metric will be described in detail in Section 2.3.4, and will be further used in the superuser route design.

In Section 2.3, we also verify the presence and stability of geo-community structure in realistic MSNet traces, and then show the efficiency of geo-centrality characterizing the "dynamic user density" of communities.

2.2.2 Big Picture

We consider a following scenario: a salesman is about to advertise his products to on-campus customers (e.g. faculty, staffs, and students). He has to physically move around the campus to transmit advertisements via his smartphone to users'. He is trying to decide his route, aiming to broadcast the ads to mobile users as soon as possible.

In our data broadcast scheme, the users in MSNets are classified into two categories, (*a*) Regular users, or simply, the users that move based on their social lives. These users are potential data receivers from the superuser. The movements of the users are not controllable; (*b*) A single special user called superuser (e.g. the salesman) that aims to broadcast data to regular users in the network. In this chapter, we only consider *one-hop* data broadcasting from the superuser to regular users. Opportunistic transmission between regular users are not our focus. This is because rational users can be expected to behave selfishly and need incentive to cooperate in human society, and we believe the incentive schemes in MSNets deserve separate studies. Hence, we leave them for future work, and discuss more in Section 2.7.3. The data broadcast problem is, therefore, how to design a superuser route to facilitate data broadcasting most effectively. To solve such a problem, we should focus on answering the following questions:

- What is the appropriate metric for measuring the dynamic user density of geo-communities?
- Given the dynamic user density of each geo-community, how the superuser decide which geo-communities it can stay, and for how long, respectively?

Generally speaking, the exploitation of both social and geographic regularities of user mobility in MSNets will definitely facilitate the calculation of geo-centrality metric, i.e., the dynamic user density of geo-community. As a matter of fact, users in MSNets always move around several well-visited geo-communities, and their sojourn times at each geo-community remain stable over time. Hence, we employ a Markov process to model user mobility in the network, where the geo-communities are represented as Markovian states.

Through analyzing the Markov model, we can compute each user's steady-state probability distribution over geo-communities, and further propose geo-centrality, the cumulative contact probability between community and users, for each geo-community to measure its dynamic user density. Suppose the whole network is composed of a certain number of geo-communities, the problem of superuser route design is then turned to: How should the superuser choose geo-communities and allocate waiting times accordingly? Figure 2.1 gives an illustration of our geo-community-based data broadcast scheme.

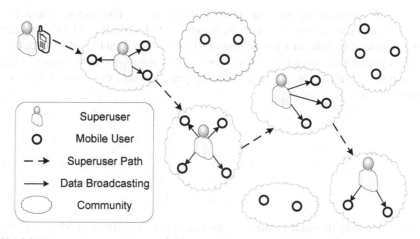

Fig. 2.1 Diagram demonstrating our geo-community-based data broadcast scheme in MSNets

Table 2.1 Trace Summary

Trace	MIT Reality	Infocom 06	CoSphere
Device	Smart Phones	iMote	Smart Phones
Network type	Bluetooth	Bluetooth	Cellular, 802.11 and Bluetooth
Duration (days)	246	3	42
Granularity (minutes)	5	2	5
No. of devices	97	78	12

2.2.3 Optimization Objectives

We consider two cases: (1) The superuser aims to minimize the total duration of route T under the constraint of a certain dissemination ratio, which corresponds to *time-sensitive superuser*. For example, the salesman tries to use less time to advertise the product to a certain number of people; (2) The superuser aims to maximize the dissemination ratio p before a certain deadline, which corresponds to *dissemination-ratio-sensitive superuser*. In this case, the salesman tries to advertise the product to more people within working time.

In both cases, the superuser route design scheme follows a utility-based approach. The superuser route comprises some geo-communities and the corresponding waiting times. Suppose that the whole network is composed of a certain number of geo-communities, and the superuser can immediately transmit data to all the users within the geo-community where the superuser is stopping. The utility u_i of geo-Community i describes its potential contribution to the superuser's data dissemination. From a statistic perspective, the number of users to whom the superuser transmits data at geo-Community i does not decrease with increasing t_i, which indicates the superuser's waiting time at geo-Community i. In other words, $u_i(t_i)$ is a non-decreasing function of t_i. However, the key point is that the increment of $u_i(t_i)$

with t_i is different among geo-communities, therefore we should then allocate the limited time to geo-communities with higher gradient of $u_i(t_i)$. It will be shown later that the associated utility of a geo-community is strongly related to its geo-centrality.

The optimization objective for the *time-sensitive superuser* is to minimize the total duration of the route T, and at the same time guarantee the required dissemination ratio p.

$$\min T$$

$$s.t. \sum_{i=1}^{J} u_i(t_i) \geq p \tag{2.1}$$

$$t_i \geq 0, 1 \leq i \leq J,$$

where J indicates the total number of geo-communities in the network. Note that T represents the total duration of the route, which includes waiting time T_w and traveling time T_t, i.e., the total route time $T = T_w + T_t$, where $T_w = \sum_{i=1}^{J} t_i$. Suppose only waiting time contributes to the superuser's data dissemination, Eq. (2.1) can be solved by independently minimizing T_w and T_t, which correspond to a convex optimization problem and a Traveling Salesman Problem (TSP), respectively.

On the other hand, the optimization objective for the *dissemination-ratio-sensitive superuser* is to maximize the dissemination ratio p, under the constraint of a certain route duration T.

$$\max p = \sum_{i=1}^{J} u_i(t_i)$$

$$s.t. \sum_{i=1}^{J} t_i + T_t(t_0, t_1, \ldots, t_J) \leq T \tag{2.2}$$

$$t_i \geq 0, 1 \leq i \leq J,$$

where $T_t(t_0, t_1, \ldots, t_J)$ indicates the total traveling time of the superuser traversing between the chosen geo-communities (i.e., $\{i | i \in \bigcup_{1 \leq i \leq J}(t_i > 0)\}$). The constraint contains an integer variable, hence the route algorithm of the *dissemination-ratio-sensitive* superuser is more complicated than that of the *time-sensitive* one.

The two above optimization problems can be solved with the methods we outline in Section 2.5.

2.3 Trace-based Analysis on Mobile Social Networks

In this section, we explore both social and geographic regularities of user mobility in MSNets based on realistic trace study, and further propose the concepts of geo-community and geo-centrality.

2.3.1 Experimental Traces

We study the characteristics of user mobility on three sets of MSNet traces. We believe that the chosen traces cover a rich diversity of environments, from crowded conference sites (*Infocom 06*) [99] to quiet university campuses (*MIT Reality* and *CoSphere*) [100, 101], with experimental periods from a few days (*Infocom 06*) to almost one year (*MIT Reality*). The three traces are summarized in Table 2.1.

We choose traces containing static Access Points (APs) because APs have geography-related properties. Specifically, we use the *syslog* data for mobile users' association patterns to APs. From these *syslog* messages, the mobility of each user is extracted in the form of a series of two tuples (AP name and the timestamp when the association with this AP occurs). For simplicity, we classify more than 30,000 APs in the *MIT Reality* trace into 50 geo-locations. In both *Infocom 06* and *CoSphere*, the neighborhood of each AP corresponds to one geo-location.

2.3.2 Geographic Regularity of User Mobility

We investigate whether or not, and to what extent, user mobility behaviors in realistic MSNets correlate in time and space. From a user-centric view, we define the "contact geo-location set" as follows:

Definition 1. *The **Contact geo-Location Set (CLS)** of a user i during time period $[t_1, t_2]$ is a geo-location set $\mathscr{L}_i$, where for any $1 \leq j \leq |\mathscr{L}_i|$, the cumulative sojourn time $T_{i,j}$ of user i at geo-location j is larger than λ, which is a pre-defined threshold.*

Note that the introduction of λ is in order to exclude the effect of pass-by geo-locations to some extent. First, we compare the similarity of user's sojourn time distributions over *CLS* based on traces collected in time intervals of different scales from the *MIT Reality* dataset, where λ is set to 0. We choose *cosine distance* as the similarity measure. In the current problem, the cosine distance $sim(\mathbf{p}, \mathbf{q})$ is defined as:

$$sim(\mathbf{p}, \mathbf{q}) = \frac{\sum_{j=1}^{J} p_j q_j}{\left(\sqrt{\sum_{j=1}^{J} p_j^2}\right)\left(\sqrt{\sum_{j=1}^{J} q_j^2}\right)} = \frac{\mathbf{p} \cdot \mathbf{q}}{|\mathbf{p}||\mathbf{q}|}, \qquad (2.3)$$

where p_j and q_j indicate a user's sojourn time at geo-location j during the two time periods under comparison. Then, $\mathbf{p} = [p_j]$ and $\mathbf{q} = [q_j]$ are the sojourn time distributions over the user's *CLS* during the two corresponding time periods, respectively. Note that $sim(\mathbf{p}, \mathbf{q})$ ranges in $[0, 1]$, with $sim(\mathbf{p}, \mathbf{q}) = 1$, indicating that the user's mobility behaviors in the two time periods are identical.

Figure 2.2(a) shows the cosine distance between monthly traces collected in a period of 2 months (October and November, 2004), where the gaps mean the corresponding users have no *syslog* in this period. It can be observed that over 85%

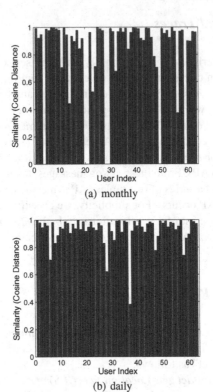

(a) monthly

(b) daily

Fig. 2.2 Similarity between users' *CLS* derived based on the *MIT Reality* traces of different time-scales

Table 2.2 Numerical Parameters on the *CLS* Size Distribution

Trace	MIT Reality	Infocom 06	CoSphere
Mean (μ)	3	1.7846	2.1818
Variance (σ^2)	1.0389	1.2464	0.9360

of active users[1] have similarity values higher than 0.9, and most of which approach 1. Figure 2.2(b) gives such a similarity measure derived based on daily traces. As the mobility data collected from the daily trace is insufficient to characterize the mobility behavior, we construct the mobility models at the daily scale by separately gathering all the *syslog* data on Monday and Tuesday during the whole 9-month experiment period. It is again observed that the similarity values are extremely high in most users. In short, the results show that users in MSNets always keep a stable movement schedule in a relatively long interval. Hence, we can extract user's past mobility characteristics to predict his/her future movement.

---

[1] Every user visits at least one geo-location during the experiment duration.

We also study the *CLS* size of each user, which represents the number of geo-locations that a user mostly move around during the experiment period. Here, λ is set as 30*min* per day to exclude the effect of pass-by geo-locations. The results in Table 2.2 show that the mean value of users' *CLS* size is 3 in the *MIT Reality* trace. On the other hand, such measures in *Infocom 06* and *CoSphere* are even lower, around 2. The low variances mean that the *CLS* size of all the users keep around the mean. Hence, it can be concluded that users in MSNets usually move around several locations instead of all over the whole network. It also demonstrate the phenomenon of skew spatial distributions of users in MSNets.

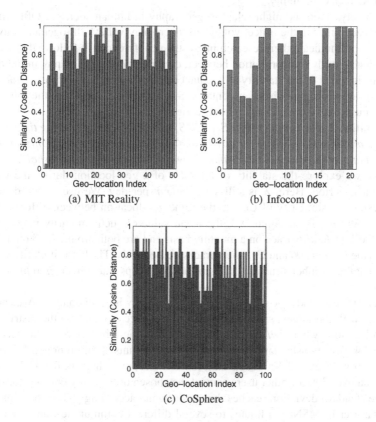

(a) MIT Reality   (b) Infocom 06

(c) CoSphere

Fig. 2.3 Average similarity of *CUS* in different time scales for each geo-location

2.3.3 Geo-Community

A community is defined as a clustering of users that are "tightly" linked to each other, either by direct linkage or by some "easily accessible" users that can act as intermediaries. Members of a community usually share interesting properties, such as common hobbies, social functions, and occupations [102]. On campus, graduate students working in the same office interact more frequently with each other; members affiliating with the same team, such as football or swimming, have such heavy interactions. In an academic conference, scholars having mutual research interest also make up a community.

Intuitively, interests might relate to geography in human society[2]: Officemates contact each other in the office; volleyball lovers play volleyball together in gyms; scholars communicate their research interests in conferences. It follows that we experimentally study the correlation between community and geography in the three datasets, in terms of the stability of "contact user set" of each geo-location and spatial distributions of pairwise user contacts. Similar to *CLS*, we define the following "contact user set" from a location-centric view:

Definition 2. *The **Contact User Set (CUS)** of a geo-location j during time period $[t_1, t_2]$ is a user set $\mathscr{S}_j$, where for any $1 \leq i \leq |\mathscr{S}_j|$, the cumulative sojourn time $T_{i,j}$ of user i at geo-location j is larger than λ, which is a pre-defined threshold.*

First, we explore the stability of the *CUS* of a geo-location during the whole experiment period. Here, λ is still set to $30min$ per day. We use cosine distance to measure the similarity of *CUS* at the same geo-location between different time periods. As seen from Figure 2.3, the mean value of such similarity measures is 0.8 in the *MIT Reality* trace on a monthly basis and are both around 0.75 on a daily scale in the *Infocom 06* and *CoSphere* traces, respectively. The high similarity values prove that the member structure of a geo-location keeps stable in an extremely long period.

Then, we also study the spatial distributions of pairwise user contacts. We choose one user with the largest size of *syslog* from the traces to analyze the distribution of geo-locations where he/she makes contact with the other users in the network. Figure 2.4 gives the standard deviation of contact counts at different geo-locations. As seen from Figure 2.4(a), such a measure is extremely high in the *MIT Reality* trace, and over 79% of other users contact the chosen user at only one geo-location, i.e., the standard deviation reaches the upper bound accordingly. The real situation is that a user in MSNets affiliates to several different communities, and then they periodically act as the different roles, respectively. Hence, a user usually contacts other users who have at least one common interest with him/her at the according geo-locations.

Therefore, a geography-related community is proposed, *geo-community*[3], to characterize the stable member structure of a geo-location in MSNets.

---

[2] Online social networks, such as Facebook and MySpace, are beyond the scope of this chapter.

[3] We will use the terms, *community* and *geo-community*, interchangeably in subsequent sections.

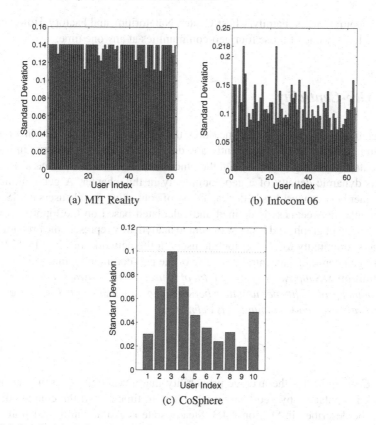

Fig. 2.4 Standard deviation of spatial distribution of pairwise user contacts over geo-locations

Definition 3. *A **geo-community** is defined as both the community which contains a clustering of users with a common interest, and the geo-location where community users contact each others mostly.*

For simplicity, we assume that one geo-location corresponds to a geo-community, and we consider the sojourn time of a participant spending at a geo-community as the time interval of his/her two consecutive contacts with different geo-locations, the former of which is the corresponding geo-community. Later, the geo-community shows its efficiency in modeling user mobility in MSNets.

A single user can be a mutual member of several different communities (people have varying roles in society). However, we consider that a user only shows one membership at any single time in this chapter. In other words, the whole network is composed of a certain number of geo-communities, where a user contacts exactly one geo-community at any one time. The user can change geo-community affiliation over time, and we assume he/she does not spend any time on the transition between geo-communities. For example, consider a father in a family, who loves Chess and swimming and works as a leader in a doll factory. He therefore affiliates to the above four geo-communities: Family, Chess Center, Natatorium, and Factory. However, he affiliates to only one of those four geo-communities at any one time.

2.3.4 Geo-Centrality

'Betweenness' centrality, which measures the extent to which a node lies on the paths linking other nodes, is currently a widely used Freeman's measure in social-based data forwarding [50] [65]. On the other hand, we use 'betweenness' to measure the dynamic density of a geo-community in this chapter. A geo-community with higher betweenness has better capability of contacting mobile users in MSNets.

Certainly, betweenness is defined and calculated based on the topology of the network contact graph, and is not sufficient to analytically represent the probabilities for a geo-community to contact mobile users in the network. Inspired by [72], we propose geo-centrality, a centrality metric of the geo-community, into MSNets:

Definition 4. *Suppose there are a total of N users in the network, and the steady-state contact probability per unit time between geo-Community i to $User_k$ is ϕ_i^k. The* ***geo-centrality*** *of geo-Community i is defined as:*

$$C_i(t_i) = 1 - \frac{1}{N} \sum_{k=1}^{N} (1 - \phi_i^k)^{t_i}, \qquad (2.4)$$

where $C_i(t_i)$ indicates the average probability that a randomly chosen user in the network is contacted by geo-Community i within time t_i, and the computation of ϕ_i^k will be described in Section 2.4.3. Steady state is a situation in which all state variables are constants in spite of ongoing processes that strive to change them. The unit time means we focus on the discrete time system in our work. A user being contacted by a geo-community indicates that the user affiliates with that community, e.g., the father is contacted by the geo-community Factory when he's working.

To show the effectiveness of geo-centrality metric in characterizing the capability of a geo-community to contact mobile users in the network, we choose a geo-community in the *Infocom 06* trace and run it 100 times with a random starting time for statistical convergence. The statistical results on the number of contacted users show the trend to form the red line in Figure 2.5(a), where the geo-centrality curve is drawn with the unit time equal to 3 minutes. The comparison results prove the feasibility of using geo-centrality to represent the dynamic user density of a geo-community. We further draw the geo-centrality curves of all the geo-communities in the *Infocom 06* trace in Figure 2.5(b), where it can be observed that geo-communities have the heterogenous capability to contact users, i.e., spatial user distributions over geo-communities are very diverse.

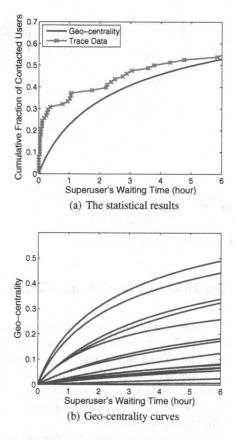

(a) The statistical results

(b) Geo-centrality curves

Fig. 2.5 Empirical study on geo-centrality in *Infocom 06*

2.4 User Mobility Model

Users in MSNets always belong to several communities, hence why they usually move around these well-visited locations (i.e., geo-communities). Therefore, we can model user mobility as a Markov process, where the states space can be represented by the set of geo-communities. In this section, we first explore the sojourn time distributions of users over geo-communities in MSNets. Based on the resulting power-law distributions, we then employ a semi-Markov model, in which the computation methods of several critical parameters are further presented. Finally, the feasibility of modeling user mobility as a semi-Markov process has been experimentally evaluated with realistic traces.

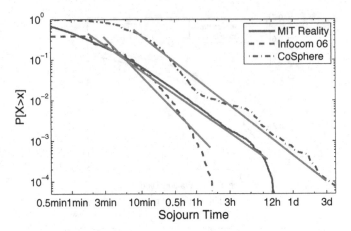

Fig. 2.6 Distributions of sojourn time for the realistic traces

2.4.1 User's Sojourn Time Distribution over Geo-Communities

We first study the distributions of user's sojourn time over geo-communities on the three traces. As seen in Figure 2.6, the sojourn time distributions approximate to the power law within a certain range (the approximate lines are drawn with red lines). Since a power law is determined by the gradient of the line on log-log graphs, the coefficient partly characterizes the sojourn time distribution of the traces. For *Infocom 06*, the coefficient is 1 in the range $[5min, 1h]$, while the distribution coefficient of *CoSphere* is 0.95 in the range $[10min, 2.5d]$.

It can also be observed that the sojourn time distributions have a heavy tail, i.e. the sojourn time decreases slowly in the tail. In the *Infocom 06* trace, around 15% of records are more than 4.5 minutes, and over 5% are larger than 12 minutes; for the *MIT Reality* trace, 20% of contacts last more than 3 minutes, and 5% are longer than 13 minutes.

Since user's sojourn time over geo-communities follows power-law, but not exponential distributions, we employ semi-Markov process instead of continuous-time Markov chain to model user mobility in MSNets. Different from standard continuous-time Markov chain, a semi-Markov process allows for arbitrary distributed sojourn times and can be considered as a process with an embedded Markov chain, where the embedded points are the time instants when a user associates him/herself with a new geo-community. Semi-Markov process has also been used in [103] and [97] to model user mobility. However, the real situation behind such mobility patterns of mobile users has never been explored. Moreover, they lay particular attention to the transient behaviors of the model and have not considered any social network concept. In this chapter, we focus on the steady-state behaviors of the model to compute geo-centrality of communities, and further design algorithms described in Section 2.5 for the superuser route.

2.4.2 Time Homogeneous Semi-Markov Model

We consider a user's mobility as a Markov renewal process $\{(X_n, T_n) : n \geq 0\}$, where T_n is the time instant of the n-th transition ($T_0 = 0$) and $X_n \in \mathbb{S}$ is the state at the n-th transition. The states space is represented by the set of geo-communities $\mathbb{S} = \{1, 2, \ldots, J\}$. A user that moves between two geo-communities transfers in the Markov process between the corresponding two states. We assume the transition probabilities between states have the Markov memoryless property, which means that the probability of a user to transfer from state X_n to state X_{n+1} is independent of state X_{n-1}. Thus, process (X_n) is a standard Markov chain. Random variable $T_{n+1} - T_n$ describes the geo-communities sojourn time. Then, the associated time homogeneous semi-Markov kernel Q is defined by:

$$\begin{aligned} Q_{ij}(t) &= Pr(X_{n+1} = j, T_{n+1} - T_n \leq t | X_n = i) \\ &= p_{ij} H_{ij}(t), i, j \in \mathbb{S} \end{aligned} \tag{2.5}$$

Suppose $P = [p_{ij}]$ is the transition probability matrix of the embedded Markov chain, where the transition probability from state i to state j is

$$p_{ij} = \lim_{t \to \infty} Q_{ij}(t) = Pr(X_{n+1} = j | X_n = i).$$

We also derive the sojourn time probability distribution in state i regardless of the next state.

$$D_i(t) \triangleq Pr(T_{n+1} - T_n \leq t | X_n = i)$$

Note that the distribution of the sojourn time, $D_i(t)$, during which the user is associated with geo-Community i before his/her next transition takes place can be expressed as

$$D_i(t) = \sum_{j=1}^{J} Q_{ij}(t).$$

With the transition probability matrix P and the sojourn time distribution $D_i(t)$ of the above semi-Markov process, we can characterize user mobility in MSNets. Section 2.4.3 describes how to derive these probabilities from mobility history of the available traces and further introduces the computation of steady-state probability distribution ϕ_i^k (proposed in *Definition 4.*) over communities for users.

2.4.3 Steady-state Probability Distribution over geo-Communities

Each user has his/her own spatial distribution that reflects his/her own mobility trajectory. We therefore model the semi-Markov process on each user separately, in order to compute the steady-state probability distribution ϕ_i of each user. Without loss of generality, we illustrate how to compute $User_k$'s steady-state probability distribution $[\phi_i^k], i = 1, 2, ..., J$, a $1 \times J$ vector. To determine the steady-state probability distribution $[\phi_i^k]$ of $User_k$, we need to compute two parameters first: the *transition probability matrix* P^k and the *sojourn time probability distribution matrix* $D_i^k(t)$. In this section, we describe a method to determine the two parameters using user mobility history, and then propose how to compute ϕ_i^k with the two parameters.

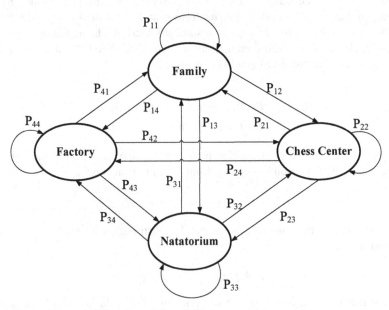

Fig. 2.7 Transition probability chart of $User_k$'s Markov model

2.4.3.1 Transition Probability Matrix

Suppose the transition probability matrix of the embedded Markov chain for $User_k$ is P^k. Figure 2.7 shows the example of transition probability matrix for the father mentioned in Section 2.3.3 that visits four geo-communities: Family, Chess Center, Natatorium, and Factory.

At any one of those geo-communities, the user could pick to reside for a while or move to another geo-community according to its preferred probability. Those mobility probabilities constitute the transition probability matrix P^k.

$$P^k = \begin{pmatrix} p_{11}^k & p_{12}^k & p_{13}^k & p_{14}^k \\ p_{21}^k & p_{22}^k & p_{23}^k & p_{24}^k \\ p_{31}^k & p_{32}^k & p_{33}^k & p_{34}^k \\ p_{41}^k & p_{42}^k & p_{43}^k & p_{44}^k \end{pmatrix}$$

We now define the P^k probabilities as follows:

Definition 5. *The transition probability p_{ij}^k that $User_k$ moves from geo-Community i to geo-Community j is defined as the observed transition frequency:*

$$For\ each\ i \neq j, p_{ij}^k = Pr(X_{t+1}^k = j | X_{t+1}^k \neq i, X_t^k = i),$$

$$with \sum_{j \neq i} p_{ij} = 1, and\ p_{ii} = 0$$

When we compute P^k, sojourn times are not taken into consideration. We only consider the transition between different states ($p_{ii} = 0$).

2.4.3.2 Sojourn Time Probability Distribution

Let $D_i^k(t)$ be the probability of the sojourn time at geo-Community i for $User_k$, regardless of the next geo-community, which can be calculated as follows:

$$D_i^k(u) = Pr(X_{t+u+1}^k \neq i, X_{t+u-v}^k = i, v = 0, \dots, u-2|$$

$$X_{t+1}^k = i, X_t^k \neq i), u = 1, \dots M_i,$$

where M_i represents the upper bound to the time spent in geo-Community i. We assume that when the network reaches steady state, the mobility history provides a representative sample from which the sojourn time distribution can be drawn.

In Markov process, the sojourn time is usually considered to have an exponential distribution. The use of a semi-Markov model in this chapter eliminates such constraint and can reflect the real world processes better.

2.4.3.3 Computation of ϕ_i^k

Given the transition probability matrix P^k, we can derive the *steady-state transition probability* $\pi^k = [\pi_1^k, \dots, \pi_J^k]$ by solving the following equation:

$$\pi^k = \pi^k P^k, \sum_{i=1}^J \pi_i^k = 1$$

In fact, π_i^k denotes the probability of $User_k$ being in geo-Community i at some transition instants.

Then, with the sojourn time probability distribution $D_i^k(t)$, we define the $J \times 1$ mean residence time vector $\bar{D}^k = [\bar{d}_i^k]$, where $\bar{d}_i^k$ is the mean value for $D_i^k(t)$. We can characterize user mobility by calculating the steady-state user distribution $\phi^k = [\phi_i^k]$ as follows:

$$\phi_i^k = \frac{\bar{d}_i^k \pi_i^k}{\sum_{i=1}^J \bar{d}_i^k \pi_i^k} \tag{2.6}$$

The steady-state distribution $[\phi_i^k]$ is the probability distribution of $User_k$ over geo-communities at any instant, and is the corresponding long-term average distribution of $User_k$ over geo-communities. We use ϕ_i^k to represent the contact probability per unit time between geo-Community i and $User_k$.

2.4.4 Similarity of Users' Steady-State Distributions in Different Time-Scales

We experimentally evaluate the feasibility of modeling user mobility in MSNets as a semi-Markov process. We calculate the steady-state distributions of users over geo-communities based on the *MIT Reality* traces collected in time intervals of different scales. The aim is to investigate to what extent the steady-state distributions derived from the semi-Markov model correlate in time. Both the transition probability matrix P^k and the sojourn time probability distribution $D_i^k(t)$ can be constructed as Section 2.4.3, and the steady-state distribution of users over geo-communities can then be calculated following Eq. (2.6).

We collect traces on monthly and daily bases to derive different steady-state distributions of users over geo-communities, and compare them with cosine distance as described in Eq. (2.3). Here $\mathbf{p} = [p_j]$ and $\mathbf{q} = [q_j]$ are the steady-state distributions of two semi-Markov models under comparison, respectively. Table 2.3 gives the above similarity measure between steady-state distributions derived based on traces of *MIT Reality* in different time-scales. The monthly traces are collected in a period of 7 months (28-week period) between 19 September, 2004 and 4 March, 2005. It can be observed that the closer in time the two monthly traces, the more similar the corresponding two steady-state distributions, though there exist some exceptions. For example, the cosine distance becomes much smaller when *m4* is involved. This is because *m4* corresponds to the period of *winter break* (from 12 December, 2004 to 8 January, 2005). This administrative event on campus affects the user mobility dramatically. It is again confirmed by daily traces that the high similarity of user mobility between each day of a week. An interesting phenomenon is that *Friday* has a lower similarity with other days, since people always have fun on Friday night.

The results verify that users in MSNets always keep a relatively stable steady-state probability distributions over geo-communities, with occasional short-term fluctuations. Therefore, modeling user mobility in MSNets as a time-homogeneous semi-Markov model is appropriate as far as the long-term movement behavior is concerned.

Table 2.3 Similarity between steady state distributions $[\phi_i^k]$ derived based on *monthly/daily* traces

Monthly	m2	m3	m4	m5	m6	m7
m1 v.s.	0.9693	0.9405	0.3183	0.8366	0.9924	0.9270

Daily	Mon	Tue	Wed	Thu	Fri	Sat
Sun v.s.	0.7077	0.7347	0.6937	0.6700	0.2898	0.5709

2.5 Designing Algorithms for the Superuser Route

In this section, we investigate how the superuser controls its mobility trajectory to meet mobile users in the network as soon as possible. We start with describing the key idea behind this process. Later, we describe the route design algorithms in detail.

The main difficulty in designing a superuser route for MSNets is that we cannot correctly predict the location of the users (a user may affiliate with several geo-communities), and hence it may not be possible to deterministically position the superuser to contact a certain regular user. However, if the steady-state probability ϕ_i^k of the presence of $User_k$ in geo-Community i (he/she belongs to that geo-community) is non-zero, then we can contact $User_k$ with certainty if we wait in geo-Community i long enough. This probability approaches 1 only as the waiting time approaches infinity. Obviously, we cannot afford to wait for an infinite amount of time, hence we cannot afford to contact the mobile users with certainty. However, it is possible to meet the users with a desired probability by waiting a finite amount of time at a geo-community, as long as the steady state probability of user presence in that geo-community is substantial such that the desired meeting probability is modest (i.e., large but not approaching 1).

Since we have the knowledge of the geo-centrality $C_i(t_i)$ for each geo-Community i in the network, our next step is to choose waiting times $t_i (\geq 0)$ at each geo-Community i, and order these geo-communities together to form a tour.

2.5.1 Static Route Algorithm

The total duration T of the superuser route has two components: (a) Waiting time T_w: The sum of waiting times at the chosen geo-communities; (b) Traveling Time T_t: The total time that the superuser spends traveling between geo-communities. The total route time $T = T_w + T_t$. Assuming that only T_w contributes to the superuser's data dissemination, the superuser route design algorithm can be broken into two subproblems: finding a good set of geo-communities and their corresponding waiting times, and ordering these geo-communities together to form a tour.

2.5.1.1 Time-sensitive Superuser

min-T-SRA In this algorithm, the superuser aims to minimize the total duration of the route T under the constraint of a certain dissemination ratio. We can look at the two steps 'choosing appropriate geo-communities' and 'constructing a path through them' independently. Since we have the knowledge of the geo-centrality function of geo-Community i ($1 \leq i \leq J$), our next step is to choose waiting times t_i corresponding to each geo-Community i, so that the total dissemination ratio for the superuser approaches p. Obviously, the geo-communities with $t_i \neq 0$ are selected as the stopping sites of the superuser. Clearly, we want to minimize the total waiting time. The corresponding optimization problem is as follows:

$$
\min \sum_{i=1}^{J} t_i
$$
$$
s.t. \sum_{i=1}^{J} C_i(t_i) \geq p \tag{2.7}
$$
$$
t_i \geq 0, 1 \leq i \leq J
$$

From Eq. (2.4), $C_i(t_i)$ is the sum of the logarithmic functions. Eq. (2.7) then becomes a convex optimization problem. Such a problem can be solved by *interior-point methods*, which are always used for solving the following optimization problems that include inequality constraints:

$$
\min f_0(x)
$$
$$
s.t. f_i(x) \leq 0, 1 \leq i \leq m,
$$

where $f_0, \ldots, f_m : \mathbf{R}^n \to \mathbf{R}$ are convex and twice continuously differentiable. The convex optimization problem is solvable, i.e., an optimal $x^\star$ exists [104]. Obviously, our optimization satisfies the required condition. Since there is only one inequality constraint in Eq. (2.7), we can transform the inequality into the objective function, then the optimization problem becomes an unconstrained problem, as follows:

$$
\min f_0(x) + \sum_{i=1}^{m} -(1/t) \log(-f_i(x))
$$

To solve the above unconstrained problem, the *barrier method* can be employed, which is based on solving a sequence of unconstrained minimization problems, using the last point found as the starting point for the next unconstrained minimization problem. In other words, we compute $x^\star(t)$ for a sequence of increasing values of t, until $t \geq m/\varepsilon$, which guarantees that we have an ε-suboptimal solution of the original problem. We refer the reader to [104] for further details.

Algorithm 1 Greedy Adaptive Route Algorithm for Time-sensitive Superuser (*min-T-GARA*)

1: $\mathbb{G} \leftarrow \varnothing; \mathbb{U} \leftarrow \mathbb{S}; T$
2: Compute $C_i'(0)$ for every $i \in \mathbb{S}$
3: Stop at the geo-community with maximal $C_i'(0)$
4: **for** $(t = 1; t < T; t++)$ **do**
5:     **if** $User_k \in Community_{cur}$ **then**
6:        $\mathbb{G} \leftarrow \mathbb{G} \bigcup User_k$
7:     **end if**
8:     $\mathbf{a}[i] = \bar{C}_i'(0), 1 \le i \le J, i \ne cur$
9:     $temp = \mathbf{a}[j] = \max \mathbf{a}$
10:    **if** $(\bar{C}_{cur}'(t_{soj}) \le temp) \wedge (\bar{C}_j(T - t - t_{cur,j}) \ge (\bar{C}_{cur}(T) - \bar{C}_{cur}(t_{soj})))$ **then**
11:       Move to Community j
12:    **else**
13:       Stay at the current community
14:    **end if**
15: **end for**

Once we have determined the geo-communities, we order them so as to minimize the length of the route. This amounts to the Traveling Salesman Problem (TSP) whose exact solution is NP-hard. TSP solvers like Concorde [105] can solve the problem accurately for a few hundred points within minutes. If the number of points is large, then we can choose any of the available approximation algorithms [106] that exist for TSP.

2.5.1.2 Dissemination-Ratio-Sensitive Superuser

max-p-SRA In this case, the concrete objective is to design a superuser route to maximize the dissemination ratio p before a certain deadline. Since geo-centrality characterizes the *utility* of a geo-community to the superuser's data dissemination, we can plug Eq. (2.4) as u_i into Eq. (2.2). Accordingly, the optimization problem is as follows:

$$\max p = \sum_{i=1}^{J} C_i(t_i)$$

$$s.t. \sum_{i=1}^{J} t_i + T_t(t_0, t_1, \ldots, t_J) \le T \tag{2.8}$$

$$t_i \ge 0, 1 \le i \le J,$$

The constraint of Eq. (2.8) contains integer variables, then the solution is NP-hard. However, this problem can be simplified as a knapsack problem. An intuitive approach [107] would be to consider the *geo-centrality to traveling time ratio* e_i of each geo-community, which is also called the efficiency of a community with

$e_i = \frac{C_i'(t)|_{t=0}}{t_{cur,i}}$, where $C_i'(0)$ indicates the gradient of $C_i(t_i)$ at $t_i = 0$, and $t_{cur,i}$ represents the traveling time from the current community to Community i, and try to select the communities with highest efficiency into the knapsack. The superuser can wait at each chosen community until the increment of geo-centrality descends below a certain threshold δ. Obviously, the set of communities generate the highest centrality while consuming the shortest traveling time in total.

Note that a user can belong to several communities, which introduces a potential *overlap* among *CUS* of geo-communities in the network. Consider the example of the father described in Section 2.3.3, who is the mutual member of four communities, which means his steady-state distribution contributes to the geo-centrality of all these four geo-communities. However, the superuser route is comprised of some *ordered* geo-communities, i.e., in the form of geo-community scheduling. It is possible that the superuser has already delivered the data to the father in one of those geo-communities, such as the Factory. Then, the contribution from the father to the other three communities should be excluded, because the superuser does not need to disseminate data to the same users more than once. That's why we define the above algorithms for the superuser route design as *Static Route Algorithm (SRA)*, and further propose a *Greedy Adaptive Route Algorithm (GARA)*, which introduces the scheme of updating geo-centrality for communities each step, in terms of all the non-contacted users in the network.

2.5.2 Greedy Adaptive Route Algorithm

In this algorithm, we also choose geo-centrality as the community's utility, but it instead computes geo-centrality of *non-contacted users* for each community repeatedly. In other words, *GARA* overcomes the overlap of *CUS* among geo-communities by updating the current geo-centrality of each community dynamically.

Throughout the rest of this section, we use the following notation. Given a collection of geo-communities $\mathbb{S} = \{1, 2, \ldots, J\}$ over a domain of users $\mathbb{M} = \{1, 2, \ldots, N\}$. Let $\mathbb{G}$ be a collection of *contacted* users (i.e., the users who have already received the data from the superuser). Given $C_i(t_i)$ as the geo-centrality function of geo-Community i during waiting time t_i, we further propose $\bar{C}_i(t_i)$ to denote such centrality of *non-contacted* users covered by geo-Community i (i.e., facing users not covered by set $\mathbb{G}$).

Algorithm 1 shows the details of *GARA* for *time-sensitive superuser* (i.e., *min-T-GARA*), where T represents the time constraint for the superuser route, the subscript *cur* indicates the current community where the superuser stays. t_{soj} is the waiting time at the current community, and $t_{cur,j}$ indicates the traveling time from the current community to Community j, which is a constant and known by the superuser as described before. $\bar{C}_i'(0)$ stands for the gradient of $\bar{C}_i(t_i)$ at $t_i = 0$. Note that *min-T-GARA* can be easily changed to *max-p-GARA* by modifying *Step. 4* to the constraint of dissemination ratio.

We elaborately illustrate *Step* 8. − 11. in Algorithm 1. Intuitively, *GARA* aims to maximize the sum of centrality within the total duration of superuser route. Obviously, the superuser will choose the geo-community with maximal $C_i'(t)|_{t=0}$ as the first stop. What matters is *if* and *when* the superuser should move to other geo-communities. Without loss of generality, we consider the condition of two geo-communities in the network. As shown in Figure 2.8, suppose there are two geo-communities with $C_1'(t)|_{t=0} > C_2'(t)|_{t=0}$, and the traveling time $t_{1,2}$ between two geo-communities is a constant given a superuser speed.

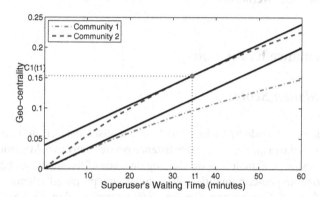

Fig. 2.8 Sketch illustrating the optimal transition time instant t_1

Assumptions on *when* and *if* the superuser should move to the other geo-communities are:

C1: The waiting time t_1 for the superuser stays at geo-Community *1* before leaving for geo-Community *2* is

$$C_1'(t)|_{t=t_1} = C_2'(t)|_{t=0} \tag{2.9}$$

C2:

$$C_2(t_2) \geq C_1(T) - C_1(t_1) \tag{2.10}$$

Theorem 2.1. Suppose assumptions C1-C2 hold, then the total centrality will achieve maximum within time constraint T.

C2 is obvious, since if the travel cost of moving to the other geo-community is less than the total utility gain, the superuser should move; otherwise, the superuser would better stay at the current geo-community. However, the optimal transition time instant (Eq. (2.9)) is proved as follows:

Proof. The time constraint for the superuser is $T = t_1 + t_2 + t_{1,2}$, $T' = T - t_{1,2}$, then $t_1 + t_2 = T'$. Since T and $t_{1,2}$ are constants, T' is a constant.

It is easy to show that $\frac{\partial C_1(t_1)}{t_1} = \frac{\partial C_2(T'-t_1)}{t_1}$ since $C_1'(t)|_{t=t_1} = C_2'(t)|_{t=0}$, then $\frac{\partial C_1(t_1)}{t_1} + \frac{\partial C_2(t_2)}{t_2} = 0$, and further $\frac{d(C_1(t_1)+C_2(t_2))}{dt_1} = 0$. The total centrality function

$C = C_1(t_1) + C_2(t_2)$, which is a concave function and will achieve maximum at $\frac{dC}{dt_1} = 0$.

Note that the prerequisite of Theorem 2.1 is that the two geo-communities have unchanged centrality functions, whereas *GARA* faces the dynamic centrality of geo-communities. However, the algorithm can guarantee the maximal total utility for the whole system at the transition time instant (i.e., t_i).

In contrast to *SRA*, *GARA* can overcome the overlap among geo-communities in the network by facing non-contacted users each step, but the trade-off is introducing more computational overhead.

2.6 Performance Evaluation

2.6.1 Simulation Setup

Our evaluations are conducted with Matlab on a realistic dataset, *Infocom 06*, with AP locations on the map. We extract the distance between any two APs from the map of conference site[4], and treat it as the moving distance of the superuser between the two corresponding geo-communities. We compare the proposed schemes (*SRA* and *GARA*)[5] with the following two Message-Ferry based routing schemes [91] [95] for *time-sensitive (min-T)* and *dissemination-ratio-sensitive (max-p)* superusers, respectively.

- **Message Ferry moves with Restricted Random Way-point model (*MF-RRWP*)**: The ferry moves according to the random way-point mobility model, with the restriction that the way-points are only chosen from the center of each geo-community. At each way-point, the ferry pauses for exponentially distributed time with a mean of 15 minutes. Note that this ferry model can also be thought of as one where the ferry visits one geo-community after the other, at random.
- **Message Ferry moves along ordered set of way-points (*MF-ORWP*)**: In this model, we also pick the center of each geo-community as a way-point, and order these way-points so as to form a shortest possible tour using the Concorde Traveling Salesman (TSP) solver [105]. The message ferry route is in the form of traversing the ordered set of way-points repeatedly.

In the simulations, we focus on the following three metrics, which are key characteristics in data dissemination of MSNets:

---

[4] The performance is supposed to be evaluated in a larger mobile social environment, but to the best of our knowledge, the *Infocom 06* dataset is the only one who both provides the geography information of all the APs and also represents the real movements of the users (i.e., it is collected using mobile phones but not laptops). Therefore, we magnify the map of the conference site on a scale of 1:10.

[5] We set 3 minutes as time unit in *SRA* and *GARA*.

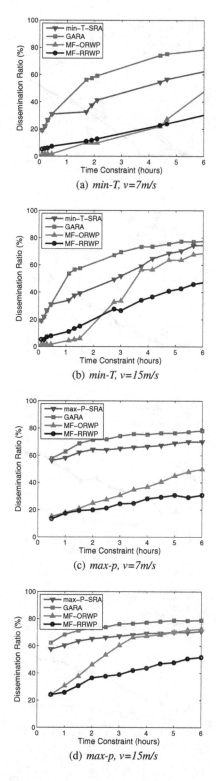

Fig. 2.9 Dissemination ratio under different superuser route schemes, and different superuser speeds

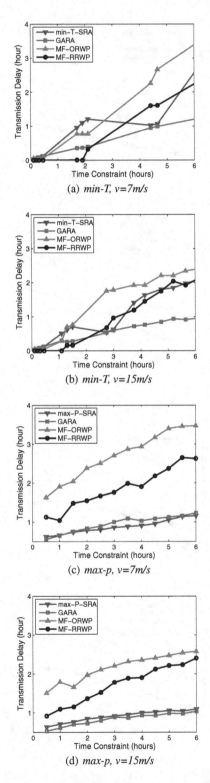

Fig. 2.10 Data transmission delay under different superuser route schemes, and different superuser speeds

- **Dissemination ratio**: the ratio of the number of delivered users to the total number of users in the network.
- **Transmission delay**: the average delay for all the delivered users.
- **Average cost**: the traveling distance of the superuser. Note that although the superuser is not limited in power supply, we still aim to maximize the energy efficiency.

2.6.2 Performance Comparison

In general, *min-T-SRA* and *max-p-SRA* both select geo-centrality as the utility of geo-community, then they have almost the same performance improvement trend compared with other existing schemes in the respective application scenarios. Since *time-sensitive case* has been partially studied in [108], we pay particular attention to the analysis of *dissemination-ratio-sensitive* (i.e., *max-p*) case in this section.

Intuitively, reader might think that the *MF-ORWP* scheme would perform well since it covers the entire region. However, there are good reasons for its poor performance. For time constraint $T = 2h$ and the superuser speed is $15m/s$, the length of the route (tour) for *MF-ORWP* is 150km, compared with 40km, that we observed for *GARA* in the same setting. Figure 2.11 shows the high superuser overhead of *MF-ORWP*, almost equal to *MF-RRWP*, and keeps 2 times *SRA* and 3 times *GARA*. With the same speed, the longer route length means that the superuser takes a longer time on the journey, and a significant fraction of this time is spent traveling in the parts of the region that have zero or negligible probability of user presence. Note that even though the superuser covers the entire region in *MF-ORWP*, it does not cover the entire region at once, especially when the region area is very large; therefore, the users and superuser can keep missing each other. It also also could be observed from Figures 2.9(c) and 2.9(d) that the dissemination ratio of *MF-ORWP* rises remarkably as the superuser speed increases from $7m/s$ to $15m/s$.

For *MF-RRWP*, the superuser may choose random geo-communities having no mobile user, thus time spent traveling to and staying at such communities is completely futile, except for when the path to these communities intersects the region of some mobile users. Therefore, *MF-RRWP* performs almost the worst in terms of dissemination ratio, transmission delay, and average cost.

Overall, *SRA* and *GARA* both perform significantly better than the other two MF-based schemes, with higher dissemination ratios, lower transmission delays and less superuser overhead. The main reason is that we balance the traveling time and waiting time, and moreover invest waiting time at geo-communities that are more advantageous in terms of increasing the contact probability with the mobile users. It can be observed from Figure 2.9(c) and 2.9(d) that *max-p-SRA* performs almost as good as *GARA* when the time constraint T is small (30*min* in the experiment setting), since the superuser in *max-p-SRA* doesn't have enough time to visit a certain user more than once in such a short time frame. As T gets larger, *GARA* takes advantage of updating geo-centrality metrics in terms of non-contacted users.

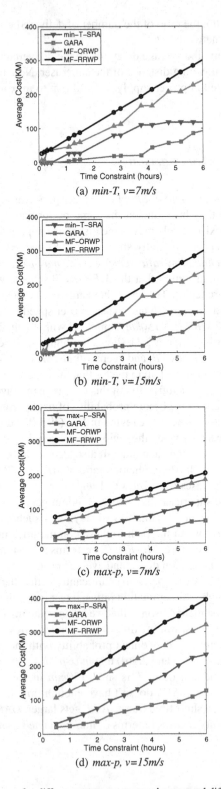

(a) *min-T, v=7m/s*

(b) *min-T, v=15m/s*

(c) *max-p, v=7m/s*

(d) *max-p, v=15m/s*

Fig. 2.11 Average cost under different superuser route schemes, and different superuser speeds

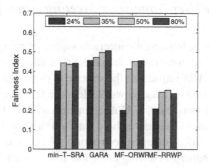

(a) *min-T, v=7m/s*

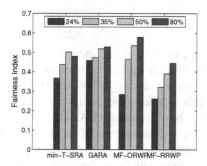

(b) *min-T, v=15m/s*

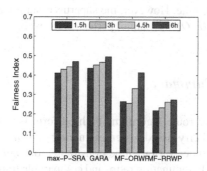

(c) *max-p, v=7m/s*

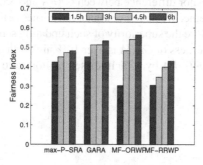

(d) *max-p, v=15m/s*

Fig. 2.12 Fairness of user-superuser meeting under different superuser route schemes, and different superuser speeds

2.6.3 Fairness of a User-Superuser Meeting Among Users

Although fairness is not an important concern in superuser route design, we want the superuser to contact more users rather than meet a small subset of users frequently. Compared with *SRA*, *GARA* introduces the scheme of dynamically updating the centrality of non-contacted users in the network. Hence, a fairness index is employed to illustrate the better performance of *GARA*, compared with *SRA* and other MF-based superuser routing schemes. The unweighted Raj Jain fairness index [109] was chosen for comparing the different superuser routing schemes. ω_i is set as the contact counts for $User_i$ to the superuser during the whole route duration. The fairness index is then defined as:

$$f(\omega_1, \omega_2, ..., \omega_N) = \frac{(\sum_{i=1}^{N} \omega_i)^2}{N \sum_{i=1}^{N} \omega_i^2}$$

A fairness index value close to 1 would indicate good fairness, whereas values significantly less than 1 will indicate lack of fairness. Figure 2.12 shows the fairness index of a user-superuser meeting of the four superuser routing schemes in the corresponding different superuser speeds and interesting objectives (*min-T* and *max-p*), respectively. It can be observed that *GARA* always performs better than *SRA* in terms of fairness because the introduction of the geo-centrality updating scheme. Note that *MF-OPWP* performs the best when the superuser speed is $15m/s$, since it covers the entire region more rapidly as the superuser accelerates. The extreme situation is that the superuser in *MF-OPWP* visits each mobile user in the network at once if its speed is infinite. However, the superuser can not afford a significantly high speed, therefore *MF-OPWP* cannot perform very well.

2.6.4 Simulation Summary

Our proposed superuser route algorithms both perform better than the other two well-known Message Ferry-based schemes in *time-sensitive* and *dissemination-ratio-sensitive* cases. Under various time constraints, our *min-T-SRA* outperforms *MF-ORWP* by 20% in dissemination ratio, and comparable transmission delay, with only 75% of its cost. The performance improvement is much better than compared with *MF-RRWP*. The major difference between *GARA* and *SRA* is introducing geo-centrality updating scheme. We also investigate the fairness of user-superuser meeting among users to explore the superiority of such updating scheme. Under different superuser speeds, the fairness of *GARA* is over 10% higher than *min-T-SRA*. Hence, *GARA* outperforms *min-T-SRA* by 15% in dissemination ratio and delay, with only 60% of its cost.

2.7 Discussions

2.7.1 Interest-based Data Dissemination

In daily life, it is possible that a superuser wants to disseminate data to a special set of users instead of all the users in the network. For example, a salesman of sport products aims to deliver the advertisements to people who love sports. Fortunately, our proposed geo-community has one-to-one correspondence with interest, hence our proposed geo-community-based broadcast scheme can deal with such an application scenario in the following way: Rather than facing all the geo-communities in the network, the superuser only considers geo-communities whose interests belong to "sports", e.g., gym, natatorium, and stadium.

2.7.2 Multiple Superuser Scheduling

Although we consider data dissemination from a single superuser, the proposed algorithms can be easily extended for multiple superuser scheduling for a higher dissemination ratio, a lower transmission delay, or a more robust dissemination performance. Even when considering the same application scenario, several salesmen cooperate to disseminate advertisements to users in the campus. They can choose the set of geo-communities and the according waiting times based on the performance requirement in a similar way. Then, the superusers trajectory planning can refer to Vehicle Routing Problems (VRP) [110] and Covering Tour Problems (CTP) [111] in vehicular networks. As a matter of fact, VRP is a generalization of the TSP, and the goal is accordingly to find a set of routes with overall minimum cost which serve all the regular user requests.

2.7.3 Incentive Scheme in Selfish MSNets

As stated in Section 2.2, one-hop broadcasting from the superuser to other users without considering opportunistic transmission among regular users has been studied, and the reason is as follows. When members of MSNets are rational entities, such as people or organizations, they can behave selfishly and aim to only maximize their own benefit without considering others' performance. In such cases, regular users in the network may not help the superuser to broadcast the data. Despite this phenomenon, existing work in selfish MSNets [112] suggests that incentive mechanism should be employed to encourage cooperation among selfish users, especially in commercial environments [113]. Therefore, we leave the study of multi-hop broadcasting as future work, and plan to exploit an incentive-based cooperation scheme to improve the performance of data dissemination in selfish MSNets.

2.8 Related Work

In the context of intermittently connected networks, e.g. DTNs, Pocket Switched Networks (PSNs), and Opportunistic Networks, a number of routing schemes have been proposed for data forwarding [50] [65] and content dissemination [51] [67]. These routing schemes exploited the fact that an end-to-end path did exist over time in intermittently connected networks, which depended on a store-carry-and-forward pattern. These works originated from Epidemic routing [89], which relied on flooding the network with messages. Although Epidemic routing can approach the performance of the optimal scheme, it is extremely wasteful of network resources. Most recent work focused on proposing routing schemes to achieve comparable performance as Epidemic routing but with a lower cost, which was measured by the number of relays needed for forwarding. Spray&wait [114] and its extended scheme Spray&focus [115] both selected a fixed number of data relays, while some other schemes made relay selection decisions based on the nodes' data forwarding metrics. In [50] and [116], a relay forwarded data to another node whose forwarding metric was higher than itself. Delegation forwarding [117] was a single-copy forwarding scheme, which reduced the cost by only forwarding data to the node with the highest metric. However, all of these schemes used the intrinsic mobility of the nodes in the network.

Another set of work considered the possibility of controlled mobility for network routing. They have proposed communication models where special mobile nodes (Message Ferry [91] [92], and Data MULEs [93], etc.) facilitated the network connectivity. However, these models always assumed the special nodes move with fixed routes. SCFR [94] studied a multiple-ferry scenario, and the ferry trajectory was adaptive to the actual traffic and location of destinations. Moreover, multiple relays were allowed in SCFR but with control. However, only ferries were mobile and all other nodes were static. Tariq et al. [95] aim towarded designing a customized ferry route without disturbing nodes' movements in mobile DTNs, but they laid many constraints on node mobility, and did not consider the social nature of the network. On the contrary, our data dissemination scheme exploited the social characteristics of mobile networks without any online collaboration between the superuser and regular users in the network. Though we focused on a different application (data broadcasting from the superuser to regular users), our superuser also could extend to work as a "data carrier" between regular users. As such, it strengthened research of both mobility-assisted routing schemes and even the foundations in the area of intermittently connected networks.

Independent from the routing schemes mentioned above, some research particularly focuses on studying the data forwarding metric to measure the nodes' capability of relaying. The data forwarding metric always be defined as nodes' contact capabilities with destinations [97] [116]. The realistic trace-based study showed that the nodes' capability of contacting others could be predicted based on their historical records. MaxProp [116] estimated the node contact probability based on the historical contact numbers. In recent social-based forwarding schemes, SimBet routing [50] used the ego-centric betweenness metric as utility and only forwards data to nodes with higher ones. Hui et al. considered node centrality as well as social community knowledge in [65]. In this chapter, we also employed a utility-based data broadcast scheme. Instead of designing a data forwarding metric to users, a geo-centrality metric was proposed to dynamically measure a community's cumulative contact probability with users in the network, which showed its effectiveness in the geo-community-based data dissemination setting in MSNets.

2.9 Conclusions

In this chapter, we have studied one-hop data broadcasting from a single superuser to other users in MSNets, the main idea behind is the exploitation of both geographic and social properties of regular users' mobility to facilitate data dissemination on purpose. We explore the geographic and social regularities of users' mobility from both theoretical and experimental perspectives. Based on the exploited characterization, we introduce a semi-Markov process for modeling regular users' mobility. The proposed superuser route comprises several geo-communities and the according waiting times, which are both calculated carefully based on the semi-Markov model. Extensive trace-driven simulation results show that our data broadcast schemes perform significantly better than other existing schemes. We believe that this chapter presents the first step in exploiting social and geographic properties for efficient data broadcasting in MSNets. Further research on data transmission schemes can benefit from our proposed *geo-community* concept.

Chapter 3
Data Query in MSNets

3.1 Introduction

Thanks to the popularity of personal hand-held mobile devices (e.g., MP3 players, PDAs and smartphones), people of similar interests or commonalities in intermittently-connected human networks can cooperate to establish network connectivity and communicate with each other in the absence of network infrastructure [69] [118]. Due to such ad hoc characteristics, Delay/Disruption Tolerant Networks (DTNs) [1] can be deployed in a number of critical areas, including battlefield operations, vehicular ad hoc networks and disaster response scenarios [80] [119] [120] [121].

Recently, the majority of work in DTNs (e.g., [65] [74] [89]) focus on routing schemes. However, the ability to access information rapidly and conveniently is also an important feature that DTNs should have since the ultimate goal of establishing such networks is to allow mobile users to access information quickly and efficiently. For example, soldiers in a battlefield need to access information related to commands from the general, detailed geographical map, information about enemy locations, weather information, etc. In order to bring these applications to the domain of DTNs, a search scheme is therefore required to work despite the unreliable network conditions.

Unlike traditional connected networks (e.g., peer-to-peer systems, Internet-accessible networks), designing information search schemes in DTNs has to overcome the intermittent connectivity among users. Therefore, we can borrow ideas from well-studied routing schemes in DTNs. Since wireless devices in DTNs are usually constrained by resources such as bandwidth, buffer space, and energy dissipation, there has been a growing interest in two-hop routing schemes to save resources [72] [114] [122]. In two-hop schemes, the source takes charge of selecting relays, but the relays are allowed to transmit the packet only to the destination. Therefore, two-hop routing schemes are scalable, and the source can control the energy cost in terms of the number of involved relays. With respect to information search scheme, the data for query is generally large, hence the energy concern is of special significance. Our research focuses on a two-hop information search scheme in resource-scarce DTN setting, where mobile users initialize the interest-based query and then delegate neighbors to get the relevant information back. We refer to this as *DelQue* (delegation query). *DelQue* can also be viewed as a special two-hop routing scheme that the destination is exactly the source.

Obviously, there is a tradeoff between data transmission delay and network over-head [123] [124]. However, Spyropoulos et al. [125] showed that when enough nodes were sufficiently mobile in the network, appropriate two-hop schemes could achieve good performance with respect to both delivery ratio and energy cost, and achieve comparable delays to an optimal scheme. We experimentally explored users' mobility with traces collected from a large diversity of environments (e.g., conference sites, university campus, and vehicular networks), and the results consistently show that *users' one-hop neighbors can cover most range of the whole network in a reasonable time period*. Then, the primary challenge of *DelQue* is how to define an appropriate *utility* of each neighbor to represent its capability to accomplish the task of both query and response.

To identify the best relays, *DelQue* exploits forecasting technique to predict user mobility based on semi-Markov model. A similar model has been used in our previous work [108] to analyze the active data dissemination in DTNs. However, *DelQue* centers on the transient-state scale of the model to propose a distributed unicast information search scheme, while [108] aims to characterize group's steady-state user density for a centralized broadcast scheme. Moreover, even there are some initial studies on information access in DTNs, such as PodNet [66] [126], or Pub/Sub [51] [67], they only considered the application that data items are cooperatively disseminated from sources towards possibly interested receivers, or assume publishers and subscribers are both expecting to find each others. On the other hand, *DelQue* focuses on a totally different scenario that sources initialize interest-based query and select relays considering their capability of both query and response. The works in this chapter are the following:

1. We use three datasets collected from realistic DTN environments to study the mobility range of users' one-hop neighbors. The experiment results show that enough users are sufficiently mobile in the network, which lays a solid fundamental to support two-hop information search schemes in resource-scarce mobile DTNs.
2. *DelQue* is in a two-hop and closed-loop form, i.e., relays take charge of both querying the relevant interesting information and getting it back to the source. Therefore, the energy cost can be lowered and source can ensure system performance with only local knowledge.
3. To identify the best relays, we define a socially-aware utility, instead of simple probabilistic polices, to represent neighbors' integrated capability to query the interesting information and then get it back to the source.
4. In computing user's utility from social patterns and mobility, we put forward a spatio-temporal prediction method based on semi-Markov model. In such prediction method, users only need to maintain two critical parameters instead of the entire past mobility history. Therefore, the technique is computationally lightweight, which makes it suitable for a resource-scarce mobile setting.

The remainder of this chapter is structured as follows. Section 3.2 provides an overview about network models, basic ideas and the trace-based experiment fundamental of users' high mobility. Then we elaborate the details of *DelQue* scheme in Section 3.3. Section 3.4 presents the computation of users' utilities for query, in which a spatio-temporal prediction of user mobility is employed. Section 3.5 evaluates the performance of *DelQue* scheme and spatio-temporal prediction via realistic trace-driven simulation. The last two sections present related work and conclusions, respectively.

3.2 Preliminaries and Overview

3.2.1 Network Models and Assumptions

A complete search procedure contains two steps: *query* and *response*. Users in the network generate queries over time. Each query has a specific interest (i.e., the data objects that the source aims to search) and a certain lifetime (i.e., TTL). Interests often highly relate to geography in human society, e.g., officemates contact each others in the office; basketball lovers play together in gyms; scholars discuss their research topics in conferences.

Consider a DTN with n mobile users moving among J geo-communities. In particular, we assume any two users located at a geo-community at the same time can establish contact to exchange messages, while users at different geo-communities cannot establish contact. Suppose geo-community and interest have one-to-one correspondence relationship with each other. Hence, the interest ID in a query corresponds to a geo-community ID.

We make no assumptions about the time instants when queries are generated or the time needed for transmission. Users do not possess any *a priori* knowledge of the number of users in the system or knowledge of any properties of the other users.

3.2.2 Information Search in DTNs: A Scenario

We consider the following application scenario in DTNs: *Eric* takes charge of security surveillance of a university campus. Today a dangerous place is the *College Theater* because there will show an opera. Unfortunately, *Eric* has been trapped in an urgent task so he cannot go there himself. Hence, he has to delegate his neighbors who can get there and then respond to him within working time to help. However, *Eric* aims to delegate as few friends as possible to accomplish the query task.

Fig. 3.1 gives the *DelQue* solution to the above example. Located at the same geo-community (*Office*) with *Eric* are *Rachel*, *Kris*, *Jerry* and *Thomas*. Based on the history mobility information, *Eric* predicts that within working time *Jerry* and

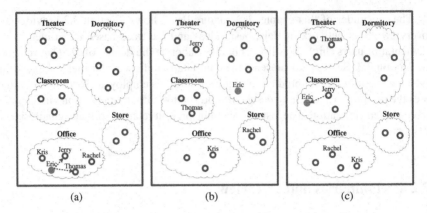

Fig. 3.1 An example to illustrate the process of *DelQue*. The dashed line stands for forwarding packets.

Thomas have better query and response performance than all the other users in the *Office*. Therefore, *Eric* forwards the query to *Jerry* and *Thomas*. In this scenario, *Jerry* goes to the *College Theater* geo-community later (Fig. 3.1(b)) and then meets *Eric* in *Classroom* for information response (Fig. 3.1(c)).

Note that the above stated story is a representative example of how *DelQue* scheme works. It does not mean *DelQue* only applies to this scenario. As a matter of fact, *DelQue* can be easily used in data query from a special data center, i.e., score query from a certain department, etc.

3.2.3 The Basic Idea

The basic idea of our approach is to develop social-based metrics based on the probabilities of users arriving destination geo-community to query the interesting information and then getting it back to the source. Based on the social-based metrics, we formulate the relay selections as a knapsack problem:

$$\min \sum_{i=1}^{n} x_i$$
$$s.t. \sum_{i=1}^{n} u_i x_i \geq U$$

(3.1)

where $x_i \in \{0,1\}$ represents whether $User_i$ is selected as the relay, and the constraint U indicates that the selected relays should satisfy the performance requirements of the source in terms of query ratio and transmission delay. Note that cost-aware relay selection schemes always employ such knapsack problem [72].

Table 3.1 Basic statistics of the traces

Trace	*MIT Reality*	*Infocom 06*	*San Francisco*
Device	Smart Phones	iMote	GPS Receivers
Network type	Bluetooth	Bluetooth	GPS
Duration (days)	246	3	24
Granularity (seconds)	300	120	10
No. of devices	97	78	536

Social-based metrics will be developed to calculate the utility u_i associated with each $User_i$ in the network, and the total required utility U is determined by the performance requirements of the source. The remainder of this chapter therefore focuses on answering the following questions:

1. What are the appropriate social-based metrics for *DelQue*?
2. How to calculate the utilities u_i of individual user?
3. How can the source calculate the total required utility U?

3.2.4 Trace-based Analysis on Neighbors' Mobility Range

In this chapter, we aim to develop a two-hop information search scheme. The prerequisite of two-hop schemes is that enough nodes are sufficiently mobile in the network. Although [125] presents this viewpoint, it did not study and validate the realistic environments. Next, we use the following three experimental traces collected from realistic DTNs to study the one-hop neighbors' mobility range: (1) faculty and students in the MIT campus (*MIT Reality*) [100], (2) participants of the Infocom 06 conference (*Infocom 06*) [99], and (3) cabs in the San Francisco area (*San Francisco*) [127]. Basic statistics about these three traces are listed in Table. 3.1, in which we can see that the three traces differ in scale, detection period, as well as the experiment environment.

For each trace, we divide the whole network into multiple geo-communities [108]. Fig. 3.2 shows the one-hop neighbor's mobility range of each user in various real traces. Note that we only count the active[1] communities as denominator of contacted community ratio. For the *Infocom 06* trace, almost all the users' one-hop neighbors have moved to around 90% communities in the network when time constraint $T = 12h$. As to *MIT Reality* with a larger scale and longer experiment period, the contacted community ratio can also reach 88% when $T = 20h$. A even higher ratio 100% can be observed from the *San Francisco* trace with a much shorter period $T = 1h$, since the mobility of vehicular networks is generally high. Through analyzing various realistic traces, we find that *users' one-hop neighbors can cover most range of the whole network in a reasonable time period*, which lays fundamentals for studying *two-hop* information search schemes in DTNs.

---

[1] communities ever visited by any user.

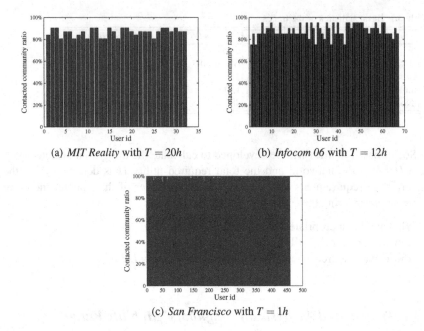

(a) *MIT Reality* with $T = 20h$ (b) *Infocom 06* with $T = 12h$

(c) *San Francisco* with $T = 1h$

Fig. 3.2 Neighbors' mobility range of each user in various realistic traces

3.3 DelQue Scheme

Suppose there are a collection of geo-communities $\mathscr{C} = \{C_1, C_2, \ldots, C_J\}$ over a domain of mobile users $\mathscr{N} = \{N_1, N_2, \ldots, N_n\}$. A query item is in the form of $< \sigma, D, T >$, where σ is the source user ID; D is the destination geo-community ID corresponding to the query interest; and T is the deadline. σ only cares the neighbors' query performance before T, which also represents the expiration time that query and data items will be removed from relays when they expire. At random times users come into the same geo-community with σ, meaning that σ is capable of delegating them to query.

Suppose the neighbor set of σ is $\mathscr{R} = \{R_1, R_2, \ldots, R_k\}$, which can be selected as query relays. p_m is the probability that the neighbor R_m can fulfill the delegation task before deadline T, i.e., query the relevant interesting information and then get it back to σ. Therefore, for R_m, let the random variable T_1 be the time for R_m to move to the destination geo-Community D, and T_2 be the time for R_m to get data back to the source σ, then the probability that σ can query the information through R_m before T is $P(T_1 + T_2 \leq T)$. Assuming that the probability density functions (PDF) of T_1 and T_2 are $f_1(t)$ and $f_2(t)$ $(t \geq 0)$, respectively, $P(T_1 + T_2 \leq T)$ is calculated through the convolution $f_1(t) \otimes f_2(t)$ as

$$p_m = P(T_1 + T_2 \leq T) = \int_0^T f_1(t) \otimes f_2(t) dt$$

$$= \int_0^T (\int_0^t f_1(\tau) f_2(t-\tau) d\tau) dt. \tag{3.2}$$

We define the required query ratio p as the fraction of query items being responded to sources. To ensure that the query ratio for σ is higher than p, the probability that all the delegated relays cannot fulfill the task should be lower than $1 - p$, i.e.,

$$\prod_{m=1}^r (1 - p_m)^{x_m} \leq 1 - p \tag{3.3}$$

where $x_m \in \{0, 1\}$ indicates whether R_m is selected as the relay. Such problem can be transformed to the knapsack formulation in Eq. (3.1) by taking logarithms on both sides of the inequality, where $u_m = \log \frac{1}{1-p_m}$ and $U = \log \frac{1}{1-p}$.

Note that when σ generates the query, it is possible that all the neighbors in contact can not accomplish the query task, then it will forward the query replica to the immediate neighbors with $p_m > \lambda$ and wait for the new neighbors until the performance requirement is achieved. We introduce λ to exclude the neighbors with lower query ratio as relays. The value of λ could be different depending on the application scenarios, and the effect of λ on *DelQue* performance is studied in Sec. 3.5.3. Note that only best-effort solution is available if $\sum_{m=1}^k u_m < U$.

The computation of p_m is detailed in Sec. 3.4.3 and based on predicting user mobility over a finite time horizon. In contrast with prior predicting algorithms, which mainly focus on estimating the probability of contact regardless of the contact time, *DelQue* presents a spatio-temporal prediction of user mobility based on a time-homogeneous semi-Markov process to determine the probabilities of contact for each time unit. The semi-Markov model does not require the storage of the entire history but only two critical parameters, *transition probability matrix* and *sojourn time probability distributions*. The technique is therefore computationally lightweight and suitable for a resource-scarce mobile setting. σ can request the above two parameters from each contacted neighbor to calculate its p_m, and decide if select R_m as relay accordingly.

We define $S(t)(0 \leq t \leq T)$ as the geo-community where the source σ stays at time t, and $S(t)$ is always a piecewise function over $\mathscr{C}$. In this chapter, we study the following two cases:

(a) **Querying for Static Source (QSS)**: The source σ stays at the original geo-community until deadline T (i.e., $S(t) \equiv S(0)$, for $0 \leq t \leq T$), which is a special case of querying for mobile source. We study this scenario firstly because this situation happens frequently in real world, e.g., *Eric* will be trapped in the office for the urgent task within the remaining working time. At the same time, the computation overhead of this situation is lower than that of querying for mobile source. *QSS* is then generalized as follows.

(b) **Querying for Mobile Source (QMS)**: The source σ moves according to a given schedule after delegation, and we assume it exactly knows where it is at any time until T (i.e., $S(t)$ is known beforehand by σ for $0 \leq t \leq T$), while users don't exchange their full schedules due to privacy etc. That is reasonable in real world, because people are usually aware of their own plan in a certain time, but would not make a clean breast of everything to others (even to family or close friends). Hence, σ has to request the relevant parameters from each contacted neighbor to compute p_m, and such calculation needs the information of σ's own following schedule $S(t)$ ($0 \leq t \leq T$). One might think if each user in the network knows its own schedule exactly, then why not ask each contacted neighbor if it goes to the destination geo-community before T. However, the simple 'yes' or 'no' can not ensure the query performance, because the delegated relays also have to get the interesting data back to the source. Without exact schedule of the source, neighbors cannot guarantee whether it can contact the source timely after querying the interesting data.

3.4 Computing Utilities from Social Patterns and Mobility

To compute a neighbor's utility to query, we should first learn its mobility characteristics. Note that the main goal of this chapter is not to propose the best synthetic
traces in realism, but to provide a lightweight forecasting technique when evaluat-
ing neighbor's utility in *DelQue* scheme for resource-scarce DTNs. Therefore, we
model user mobility in the network as a time-homogeneous semi-Markov process,
which only needs each user to maintain and exchange two parameters [97] [103].
The feasibility of such modeling has been studied in [128]. In this section, we focus
on the transient behavior analysis of the model, and present a spatio-temporal prediction method based on the devised semi-Markov model. Finally, we further propose the computation methods of social utilities for the relays selection in *DelQue*.

3.4.1 Transient Behavior of Time-Homogeneous Semi-Markov Model

User mobility is modeled as a Markov renewal process $\{(X_n, T_n) : n \geq 0\}$, where
$X_n \in \mathscr{C}$ is the state at the n-th transition and T_n is the corresponding transition
time instant ($T_0 = 0$). The state space is represented by the set of geo-communities
$\mathscr{C} = \{1, 2, \ldots, J\}$. A user that moves between two geo-communities transits in the
markov process between the corresponding states. Random variable $T_{n+1} - T_n$ describes the geo-communities sojourn time. Then, the associated time homogeneous
semi-Markov kernel Q is defined by:

$$Q_{ij}(t) = Pr(X_{n+1} = j, T_{n+1} - T_n \leq t | X_n = i)$$
$$= p_{ij} H_{ij}(t), i, j \in \mathscr{C} \tag{3.4}$$

The transition probability matrix of the embedded Markov chain is $P = [p_{ij}]$, where the transition probability from state i to state j is

$$p_{ij} = \lim_{t \to \infty} Q_{ij}(t) = Pr(X_{n+1} = j | X_n = i) \tag{3.5}$$

We also derive the sojourn time distribution in state i when the next state is j.

$$H_{ij}(t) = Pr(T_{n+1} - T_n \le t | X_{n+1} = j, X_n = i) \tag{3.6}$$

Then the sojourn time probability distribution in state i regardless of the next state is

$$D_i(t) = Pr(T_{n+1} - T_n \le t | X_n = i) = \sum_{j=1}^{J} Q_{ij}(t)$$

Now we define the time-homogeneous semi-Markov process as $X = (X_t, t \in \Re_0^+)$, with the transient distributions

$$
\begin{aligned}
\phi_{ij}(t) &= Pr(X_t = j | X_0 = i) \\
&= (1 - D_i(t))\delta_{ij} + \sum_{l=1}^{J} \int_0^t \phi_{lj}(t - \tau) dQ_{il}(\tau) \\
&= (1 - D_i(t))\delta_{ij} + \sum_{l=1}^{J} \int_0^t \dot{Q}_{il}(\tau) \phi_{lj}(t - \tau) d\tau,
\end{aligned}
\tag{3.7}
$$

where δ_{ij} represents the Kronecker δ function defined by

$$\delta_{ij} = \begin{cases} 0, & \text{for } i \neq j \\ 1, & \text{for } i = j. \end{cases} \tag{3.8}$$

3.4.2 Spatio-Temporal Prediction of User Mobility

Exploring spatio-temporal characteristics of user mobility is useful for computing user's *utility* for a certain interest query. In order to obtain the probability distribution of user's future location, we have to compute the transient distributions, $\phi_{ij}(t)$, of the semi-Markov model in the evolution equations Eq. (3.7). A numerical solution has already been proposed in [129]. Specifically, the evolution equations can be re-written for the *discrete-time* homogeneous semi-Markov process as

$$\phi_{ij}(k) = d_{ij}(k) + \sum_{l=1}^{J} \sum_{\tau=1}^{k} v_{il}(\tau) \phi_{lj}(k - \tau), \tag{3.9}$$

where $d_{ij}(k) = (1 - D_i(kh))\delta_{ij}$, $v_{ij}(k) = h\dot{Q}_{ij}(kh)$, and h is the discretization step. Using the assumption that the geo-community sojourn time random variables are independent from the embedded state transition process (X_{ij}), we derive:

$$
\begin{aligned}
Q_{ij}(k) &= P(X_{n+1} = j, T_{n+1} - T_n \le k | X_n = i) \\
&= P(X_{n+1} = j | X_n = i) \cdot \\
&\quad P(T_{n+1} - T_n \le k | X_{n+1} = j, X_n = i) \\
&= p_{ij} H_{ij}(k),
\end{aligned}
\tag{3.10}
$$

where p_{ij} represents the transition probability from state i to state j, $H_{ij}(k)$ is the probability that p_m will move from geo-Community i to geo-Community j at, or before time k. The values of p_{ij} and $H_{ij}(k)$ can be obtained from the trace data [108] as follows:

$$
p_{ij} = Num_{ij} / Num_i,
\tag{3.11}
$$

where Num_i represents the number of transitions from geo-Community i regardless of next transition, and Num_{ij} stands for the number of transitions from geo-Community i to geo-Community j.

$$
H_{ij}(k) = P(t_{ij} < k) = \sum_{n=0}^{k-1} P(t_{ij} = n)
\tag{3.12}
$$

We can also compute $D_i(kh) = \sum_{j=1}^{J} Q_{ij}(k)$. Since p_{ij} and $H_{ij}(k)$ are obtained from experimental data, $Q_{ij}(t)$ is not given in a closed form, we hence need to further approximate $\dot{Q}_{ij}(kh)$ in the expression of v_{ij} as

$$
v_{ij}(k) = \begin{cases} Q_{ij}(h), & \text{for k=1} \\ Q_{ij}(kh) - Q_{ij}((k-1)h), & \text{for k>1}, \end{cases}
\tag{3.13}
$$

In regard to this, all the parameters required in $\phi_{ij}(k)$'s computation (Eq. (3.9)) can be obtained from *transition probability matrix P* and *sojourn time probability distributions* $H_{ij}(k)$. Based on the Markov property of the underlying processes, if the state i of a user is known at time 0, then at time $k > 0$, the probability of that user being in state j is $\phi_{ij}(k)$. Therefore, distributions $\phi_{ij}(k)$ give the probability that the future location at time k of R_m will be geo-Community j considering that at time 0 the location was geo-Community i.

Upon receiving R_m's two parameters, P and $H_{ij}(k)$, σ can predict its future location from the current time to T. Therefore, each user in the network only needs to calculate and maintain the above two parameters based on its own mobility history. Obviously, *DelQue* is a lightweight information search scheme.

3.4.3 Computation of Utilities

In this section, we propose the computation of p_m defined in Sec. 3.3 for *QSS* and *QMS*, respectively.

3.4.3.1 Computing Utilities for QSS

As introduced before, the source σ stays at the same geo-Community from time 0 to T, we set the geo-community ID as S, and the interesting destination geo-Community ID is D. We focus on the *discrete-time* system, hence the expression of p_m can be re-written as

$$p_m = \sum_{k=2}^{T} \sum_{\tau=1}^{k-1} [f_1(\tau) f_2(k-\tau)], \qquad (3.14)$$

To compute $f_1(k)$ and $f_2(k)$, we introduce $\hat{\phi}_{ij}(k)$, which represents the probability that R_m is in geo-Community j at time k given his current location is geo-Community i, *without going back to Community i during time* $[0,k]$, whose computation is similar with $\phi_{ij}(k)$ and detailed as follows

$$\hat{\phi}_{ij}(k) = \sum_{l=1}^{J} \sum_{\tau=1}^{k} v_{il}(\tau) \phi_{lj}(k-\tau), j \neq i \qquad (3.15)$$

Different from Eq. (3.9), here we omit $d_{ij}(k)$ because $d_{ij}(k) = 0$ when $j \neq i$.

Once a semi-Markov mobility model has been constructed based on the association patterns of a user, we can calculate $\hat{\phi}_{ij}(k)$ by the discrete-time evolution equations given in Eq. (3.15). With $\hat{\phi}_{ij}(k)$'s, we can calculate $f_1(k) = \hat{\phi}_{SD}(k)$, $f_2(k) = \hat{\phi}_{DS}(k)$, and further calculate neighbors' p_m to select relays according to Eq. (3.3), i.e., calculate their *utility* u_m and choose relays based on Eq. (3.1).

3.4.3.2 Computing Utilities for QMS

In *QMS*, we define the relevant parameters as p'_m, $f'_1(k)$, and $f'_2(k)$. They also have the following relationships,

$$p'_m = \sum_{k=2}^{T} \sum_{\tau=1}^{k-1} [f'_1(\tau) f'_2(k-\tau)], \qquad (3.16)$$

Then, the computation of $f'_1(k)$ is the same as $f_1(k)$ in *QSS*, i.e.,

$$f'_1(k) = \hat{\phi}_{S(0)D}(k) \qquad (3.17)$$

The computation method of $f'_2(k)$ is more complex due to the introduced movement of σ, compared with $f_2(k)$ in *QSS*. According to Eq. (3.15), we can compute the probability $\hat{\phi}_{S(0)S(k)}(k)$ that R_m and σ will meet again, where $S(k)$ indicates the community where σ will stay at time k, which is known beforehand for σ according to the assumption.

For our study, we care about the probability that σ and R_m re-encounter for the first time. Note that when we talk about the first re-encounter at time k, it means that they have no contacts between $(0,k)$ anywhere. Assuming that user trajectories are independent, the probability $f_2'(k)$ of the first re-encounter at time k is defined as,

$$f_2'(k) = \hat{\phi}_{S(0)S(k)}(k) \prod_{t=0}^{k-1}(1 - \hat{\phi}_{S(0)S(k)}(t)), k > 0 \qquad (3.18)$$

Plugging Eq. (3.17) and Eq. (3.18) together into Eq. (3.16), the query probability p_m' can be obtained in *QMS*.

3.5 Performance Evaluation

In this section, we compare the performance of *DelQue* scheme with other information search schemes. Recent user-initializing information query schemes always consider *query* and *response* separately. To save buffer space, they employ well-known DTN routing schemes in query step to reserve buffer according to the query data size, and let the response be routed back along the query traces. We compare the performance of *DelQue* with such query framework with the flooding-based approach Epidemic routing [89], the mobility-based approach Spay-and-Wait [114], and the social-based approach BUBBLE Rap [65]. Since Spay-and-Wait and BUBBLE Rap are not designed for information query scheme, it's hard to apply them to *QMS* scenario. Therefore, we compare the performance of the four algorithms only in *QSS* scenario, and then experimentally explore the performance comparison of *DelQue* between *QMS* and *QSS*.

Epidemic routing relies on flooding the network with information query. Spray-and-Wait selects a fixed number of data relays (we set $L = 8$). In Bubble Rap, each query is forwarded to the destination geo-community greedily considering user centrality in a hierarchical manner based on social community knowledge.

3.5.1 Simulation Setup

The evaluation is based on the *Infocom 06* and *MIT Reality* traces. As summarized in Table. 3.1, the *MIT Reality* dataset [100] comes from an experimental trace involving 97 people for the duration of 9 months. Each participant carries a Nokia6600 smart phone with a software that periodically detects his/her peers or neighboring Access Points (APs) via the Bluetooth interfaces, and a contact is recorded when the device moves close to other users or APs. The *Infocom 06* dataset [99] contains opportunistic Bluetooth contacts between 98 iMotes, 78 of which were distributed to Infocom06 participants and 20 of which with external antennas (providing longer range) deployed at several places at the conference venue to act as APs.

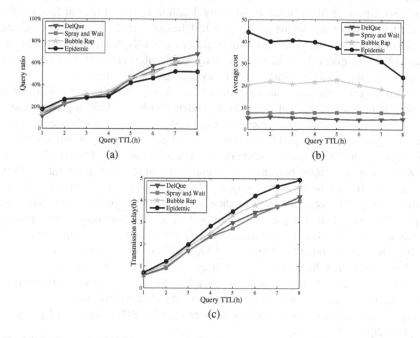

Fig. 3.3 Performance of *DelQue* compared with other search schemes: (a) Query ratio, (b) Average cost, (c) Transmission delay

In the simulations, we focus on the following three metrics, which are key characteristics in information search and data dissemination schemes of DTNs.

- **Query ratio**: the fraction of generated queries to which at least one replica is eventually responded to.
- **Average cost**: the number of relays delegated to query the interesting data, i.e., the number of replicas per generated query in the network.
- **Transmission delay**: the average duration between a query's generation and the first response of one of its replicas.

The query's source user, destination geo-community, and time of query origination are randomly generated. The sizes of query items (i.e., the interesting data sizes) are uniformly generated in the range $[10KB, 50KB]$, and each user has buffer size $1MB$. Each query has a certain TTL and will be removed after the TTL expires. All the experiments are run 500 times with randomly generated query for statistical convergence.

3.5.2 Comparison Results

We first use the *Infocom 06* dataset to compare the performance of *DelQue* with other schemes, and fix the required $p = 90\%$ and $\lambda = 0.05$. As seen from Fig. 3.3(a), the query ratio is tightly related to the query deadline T. As a matter of fact, the selected relays may not have the chance to fulfill the query tasks if the query deadline is short, due to the low contact rates among users in DTNs. Such ratio increases remarkably as the query deadline becomes longer, since the selected relays have more chances to query, and the transmission delay increases accordingly.

Since the required query ratio p cannot be achieved when the query deadline is shorter, it is possible that all the relay candidates with $\lambda \geq 0.05$ together cannot satisfy the performance requirements in Eq. (3.3), then the source hence can only copy the query to all the qualified relays with best effort. Correspondingly, *DelQue* has slightly worse performance on query ratio when T is short (< 4 hours). However, as T gets longer, *DelQue* performs better and better in terms of query ratio. When T increases from 6 to 8 hours, *DelQue* outperforms Spray-and-Wait and Bubble Rap by 10%, and keeps 30% performance advantage over Epidemic. As seen from Fig. 3.3(b), under multiple query deadline *DelQue* has a stable energy cost, which is much less than the other three existing mechanisms. When T is 8 hours, the cost of *DelQue* is only around 60% of Spray-and-Wait, 35% of BUBBLE Rap, and 20% of Epidemic. Note that the average cost of Spay-and-Wait keeps 8 because we set $L = 8$, which indicates the number of data copies distributed in the network. In terms of transmission delay, *DelQue* performs as excellent as Spray-and-Wait with multiple query deadline, and is 10% and 20% shorter than BUBBLE Rap and Epidemic, respectively.

Cost is a significant metric in DTNs, since the devices in which are always energy-scarce, and the device will be useless if the battery is exhausted. We also summarize the total size of data that each user has carried when the packet deadline is $8h$ in Fig. 3.4. Apparently, the data quantity of each user in *DelQue* is the smallest among the four algorithms. As a consequence, *DelQue* can deal with most of the query requests compared to other approaches with the same devices.

From the experiment results, it can be seen that *DelQue* can reach a slightly better query ratio and transmission delay with some well-known mechanisms, using much lower average cost. Therefore, it can be concluded that *DelQue* is an effective information access scheme.

3.5.3 Impact of p and λ

We have conducted experiments to investigate the effects of different p and λ on the query performance of *DelQue*. p (as seen from Eq. (3.3)) is the required query ratio, which is determined by the source. Upon the query ratio reaches p, the source stops choosing relays. λ is the lower-limit of the user's query requirement, i.e., the source will only choose the users whose query probabilities higher than λ.

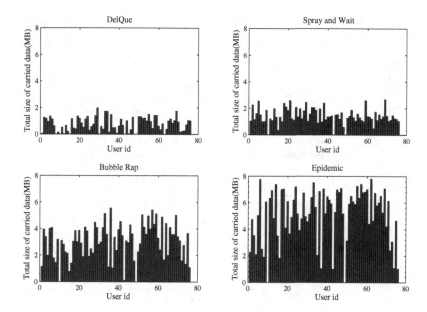

Fig. 3.4 Total size of data that each user has carried when query TTL is $T = 8h$. (For 74 active users during the period between 7am and 7pm of April 25, 2006.)

In Fig. 3.5, the effects of different required query ratio p on *DelQue* are investigated when $\lambda = 0.1$. Obviously, increasing p leads to an improvement of the query ratio, as shown by Fig. 3.5(a). When p increases from 0.5 to 0.7 and 0.7 to 0.9, the query ratios both increase by 15%-20%. Accordingly, higher p requires the source to select more query relays. When p is low, increasing p leads to a slight increment of the average cost, as shown in Fig. 3.5(b). When p increases from 0.5 to 0.7, the average cost increases by 15%-25%. Such increment becomes larger when p increases from 0.7 to 0.9, since the source will choose much more query relays with his/her best-effort to accomplish the required high query ratio. However, the actual delay remains stable among the three values of p as seen from Fig. 3.5(c), it is possibly because the query relays who finally respond the interesting information to the source are always selected.

The impact of different λ on *DelQue* are studied in Fig. 3.6 when $p = 0.9$. As seen from Fig. 3.6(a), the query ratio increases slowly with the decrease of λ. On the other hand, the average cost increases dramatically as λ decreases. Therefore, introducing λ makes *DelQue* perform more efficiently. Moreover, through tuning λ we can balance the query ratio and average cost of *DelQue* to match different application scenarios.

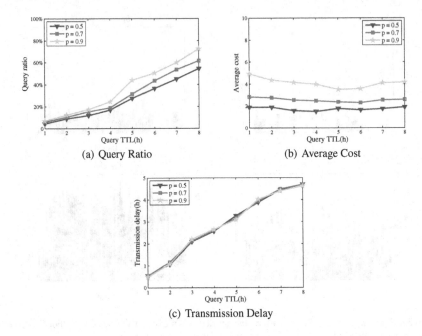

(a) Query Ratio

(b) Average Cost

(c) Transmission Delay

Fig. 3.5 Performance of *DelQue* on different p value, when $\lambda = 0.1$

3.5.4 Performance Comparison between QSS and QMS

Since other compared schemes cannot be easily extended to information query for mobile source, we compare their performance with *DelQue* in *QSS* scenario in Sec. 3.5.2. In this section, we fix the required query ratio $p = 90\%$ and $\lambda = 0.05$, and compare the performance *of DelQue* between *QMS* and *QSS* to study its flexibility and robustness.

In *QMS* scenario, source user is randomly selected as a real user in the *Infocom 06* trace. Fig. 3.7 shows the performance comparison between *QSS* and *QMS*. As seen from Fig. 3.7(a) and Fig. 3.7(c), *DelQue* performs better in *QMS* compared with *QSS* scenario in terms of query ratio and transmission delay, since the mobility of source enhances its chance of being responded to by the selected relays. In terms of the average cost, *QMS* is higher than *QSS* by over 10%, that's perhaps because a user in the dataset may always belong to and move among several geo-communities, then the users' query probability for a mobile source decreases, and the source in *QMS* needs to select more relays to accomplish the same query ratio with *QSS*.

As seen from Fig. 3.7(b), the average cost increases dramatically as the query deadline changes from 1*h* to 2*h*, and remains stable afterwards. The fact is that the source continues to choose relays to accomplish the required query ratio with best effort before $T = 2h$. Intuitively, the cost should decrease as T becomes larger, as the relays have more chance to query the interesting information. However, a user's

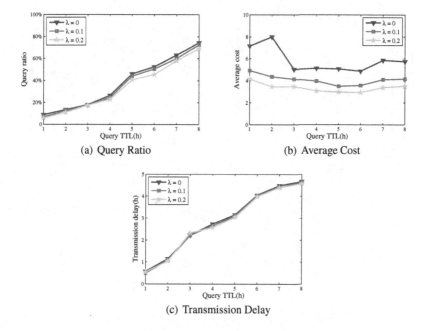

Fig. 3.6 Performance of *DelQue* with different λ value, when $p = 90\%$

query probability for the source increases slightly as T becomes larger, since a user in society doesn't move around its affiliated communities frequently. Hence, the average cost remains stable at an extremely low value (around 5).

3.5.5 Spatio-Temporal Prediction Evaluation

To compute the social utility of each neighbor, a spatio-temporal prediction method is presented. Therefore, the accuracy of such forecasting technique has a significant effect on the performance of *DelQue*. In this section, we further study the accuracy of the spatio-temporal predict method with the *MIT Reality* dataset.

3.5.5.1 Geo-Community Clustering

A major problem with the *MIT Reality* dataset is that sometimes users experience frequent re-associations between two APs in a short period of time. This phenomenon is also addressed in the Wi-Fi networks referred to as ping-pong effect. However, such phenomenon seldomly occurs in the *Infocom 06* dataset because the sparse APs deployment.

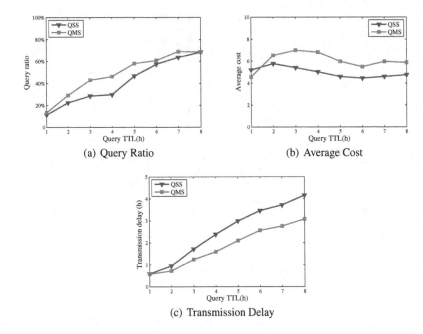

(a) Query Ratio   (b) Average Cost

(c) Transmission Delay

Fig. 3.7 Performance comparison between *QSS* and *QMS*, when $p = 90\%$ and $\lambda = 0.05$

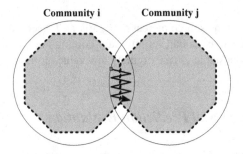

Fig. 3.8 Examples of oscillating transitions

Oscillating transitions occur when a user is geographically located among two neighboring APs. We define such oscillation as follows: For any APs i and j, if a user makes a sequence of transitions $i \rightarrow j \rightarrow i \rightarrow j$ in a short period of time. Fig. 3.8 depicts the corresponding scenario in which oscillating transitions described in the above case may occur.

Fig. 3.9 gives the cumulative distribution of users against their oscillating ratios, which is defined as the ratio of the number of oscillating transitions over the total number of transitions made by the user. When the oscillating ratio is 0.5, the cumulative distribution of users is also 0.5, which means more than 50% of the transitions have oscillating phenomenon in half of the users. The high value of oscillating ratio means this is a general phenomenon in *MIT Reality* dataset, hence it should be eliminated before modeling user mobility. In our experiment scenario, we eliminate the negative effect of oscillating AP-association by classifying the two APs together into a cluster when the frequency of transitions exceeds 4 round-trip during 8 minutes.

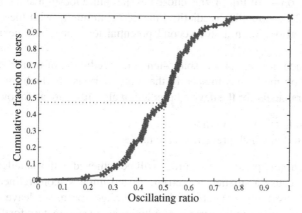

Fig. 3.9 Cumulative distribution of users against their oscillating ratios. (For 97 active users during the period between July 26, 2004 and May 5, 2005.)

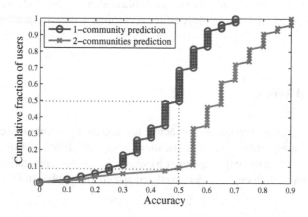

Fig. 3.10 Cumulative fraction of users against the prediction accuracy with $h = 180$ and $T_p = 1800$

3.5.5.2 Prediction Accuracy

We compare 1-community prediction with 2-communities prediction to study the accuracy of the spatio-temporal prediction, which is also to evaluate to what extent semi-Markov process is appropriate to model user mobility in DTNs. In 1-community prediction, the geo-community with the highest probability among the corresponding $\phi_{ij}(k)$ of Eq. (3.9) is chosen as the future location at the next prediction time. In 2-communities prediction, the geo-community with the next highest probability is also chosen as the second potential location at the next predicting time.

As mentioned in Sec. 3.4, the spatio-temporal prediction of user mobility based on semi-Markov model has to specify the time intervals at which predictions are made. The parameters for the devised prediction algorithm are as follows

1. h: the discretization step in time;
2. T_p: the period in which predictions are made.

In general, higher prediction accuracy will be achieved with a smaller discretization step h, because a smaller discretization step implies more refined characterization of the distribution functions. Due to limited space, we leave comparison of prediction accuracy under various combinations of parameters for future work. Fig. 3.10 shows the cumulative fraction of users against prediction accuracy under the combination of $h = 180$ and $T_p = 1800$, where the fraction of users whose prediction accuracy lower than 50% is less than 10% in 2-communities prediction and 50% in 1-community prediction. Overall, the prediction accuracy for 1-community prediction with the highest probability is reasonable (mean = 0.49), and 2-communities prediction (mean = 0.63) has slightly better performance than 1-community prediction.

3.6 Related Work

Information search and retrieval is an active research in the computer science community. There are a wide range of publications with specializations from algorithms and operations of large scale databases to search in various application scenarios, e.g., centralized search engines, decentralized search approaches in DTNs.

3.6.1 Internet Search Engines

The traditional approach to map search queries to resources through Internet is mainly based on centralized search engines (e.g., Google, MSN, and Yahoo), where the mapping is implemented by maintaining an index about the resources. The index contains keywords and maps them to sets of related resources. Centralized search engines enable one to access information by collecting and maintaining mappings of content to location. However, a hypothesis of such search engines is user's real-time Internet access authority, which can not be satisfied in people's daily life. Therefore, decentralized information search schemes emerge as the times require.

3.6.2 Decentralized Search Schemes in Unstructured Ad-Hoc Networks

Recently, decentralized search schemes in unstructured ad-hoc networks have also been studied. There are three categories of approaches for searching in such networks: flooding, random walk, and using probabilistic paths. Most flooding-based schemes use TTL (Time-to-live) to control the spread of the queries [130]. However, search-schemes based on random walks [131] [132] avoid the high cost of flooding, but cannot ensure the expected performance metric, e.g., query ratio and actual delay, due to the randomness. Specifically, we summarize several search-approaches using probabilistic paths to inspire related research in DTNs:

Hara considered the data replica allocation problem in ad hoc networks in order to improve data accessibility [133]. Three replica allocation methods have been proposed in [133], they were Static Access Frequency (SAF), Dynamic Access Frequency and Neighborhood (DAFN), and Dynamic Connectivity based Group (DCG). However, all these three methods assumed users have global knowledge of access frequencies, which may not be applicable in distributed networks. In [134], Stillerman has proposed flooding queries using limited radius and also replicating objects to improve the information retrieval latency. However, no detailed algorithms have been provided on how to replicate the objects. BubbleStorm [135] was a probabilistic search strategy, which was based on a combination of replication and probabilistic distribution of queries. Moreover, Yang and Hurson [136] presented probabilistic schemes for locating content in wireless ad-hoc networks. Based on knowledge about the query history, they used heuristics and Bayesian probability calculations to guide the dissemination of queries.

The common disadvantage of these approaches is that they always place tight demands on connectedness of the users or even consider users in networks have fixed position. However, well-connectivity cannot be ensured in DTNs, then the above approaches may not be applicable in such opportunistic networks due to the high maintenance cost of the index.

3.6.3 Information Search Schemes in DTNs

There are a few studies on web search in DTNs relying on the aid of Internet gateways. In [137], a system called *Thedu* has been proposed to enable efficient web search from a city bus. *Thedu* could be interpreted as a web proxy and collect search queries from a mobile user at the time of disconnections. Ott et al. [138] have investigated web resource retrieval in mobile DTNs via Internet gateways using well-known DTN routing mechanisms. However, we restrict our considerations to searching the mobile intermittent-connectivity environment and did not discuss interaction with infrastructure networks.

Some research on information access schemes in DTNs focused on podcasting [126], in which data dissemination was based on users' subscriptions to predefined channels. In [66], a flooding-based data dissemination scheme was proposed where data items were actively delivered from sources to interested receivers. Other existing works employed pub-sub paradigm [51] [67], in which the publisher aimed to publish the message to the interested subscribers, at the same time the subscriber also intended to retrieve the relevant message from the network. Those schemes were appropriate for the application scenarios such as distributed photo or music sharing, where users needed to be able to find content even when they did not know an unambiguous identifier.

The user-initializing information query schemes originated from *Osmosis* [139], a search mechanism for pocket switched networks, in which the queries were spread based on epidemic forwarding, and the results were routed back based on the traces that queried left while traveling between requesting node and the responding node. Most later work tried to avoid the high cost of epidemic routing at the same time to approach its query ratio. Adamic et al. [140] presented search strategies that exploited power-law degree distributions. Their method passed a search request from one node to another, choosing the neighbor with the highest degree. After the node with the maximum degree have been reached, it would be avoided, thus the search descended in the degree sequence. In [141], Pitkanen et al. have shown how caching improves efficiency with shared interest on resources using well-known DTN routing mechanisms.

One might intuitively think that evolving efficient DTN routing mechanisms would achieve high performance for information query. Most existing DTN routing algorithms aimed to find a middle ground between epidemic and wait-for-destination scheme by relying on information that can be learned during contacts. Spray-and-Wait and its extended version Spray-and-Focus [114] [116] both selected a fixed number of relays for data delivery. Some DTN routing schemes took advantage of the social behaviors of mobile users. BUBBLE Rap [65] considered social community as well as node centrality knowledge. Gao et al. studied multicast routing schemes from a social perspective in [72]. However, simply applying *directional* routing mechanism, even a two-hop one, in both query and response steps made the *bidirectional* information searching a multi-hop scheme, which introduced much overhead into the network because lots of users were involved as relays.

The work presented in this chater differs from the above stated search schemes in that *DelQue* is the first to consider *query* and *response* integratedly, i.e., the chosen relays take charge of both querying the relevant interesting message and getting it back to the source. Therefore, *DelQue* is energy-efficient and suitable for resource-scarce DTNs. Specifically, *DelQue* can lower the network cost remarkably thanks to its one-hop-delegation pattern, compared with other existing multi-hop information search schemes. Furthermore, *DelQue* is designed for information query, hence it is more flexible than other forwarding-mechanism-based query schemes, especially dealing with mobile-source scenarios.

3.7 Conclusion

In this chapter, a socially-aware information search scheme in DTNs has been proposed that mobile users initialize the interest-based query and then delegate neighbors to get the relevant information back. We refer to this scheme as *DelQue* (short for delegation query). Concretely, we consider two cases: the source is static (*QSS*) or moving after delegation (*QMS*). As a matter of fact, some existing researches also consider information search application scenarios. However, to the best of our knowledge, none of the (few) works consider the steps of query and response integratedly to save energy for resource-scarce DTNs. *DelQue* is in a two-hop and closed-loop form, i.e., relays take charge of the tasks of both query and response. Since *DelQue* does not require the selected neighbors to forward the query to other users, the network overhead can be lowered dramatically and the source can ensure system performance with only local knowledge. We also present a spatio-temporal prediction method of user mobility based on a semi-Markov model to compute the utility values, which are linked to their ability to fulfill the whole tasks. Such a lightweight forecasting technique only needs to maintain two parameters of the model, instead of the entire past history of the system, making it suitable for a resource-scarce mobile setting. Extensive realistic trace-driven simulation results show that *DelQue* has better query ratio and transmission delay with existing schemes using much less cost (in terms of the number of involved relays).

While the investigations in this chapter provide a starting point in delegation query or even information search schemes in DTNs, numerous directions become apparent which deserve further attention: We currently consider the source users only request single interest-based message, a user ,however, may aim to request multiple interest-based messages. In this work, we also assume that query items have a fixed expiration time. In real life scenarios, the expiration times of the query items may depend on the application scenarios. In addition, data-centric security design needs to be done to ensure that only legitimate users are allowed to query and respond data in an information search system operating in challenging network environments. Last but not least, we intend to build a medium sized testbed that demonstrates the *DelQue* scheme.

Chapter 4
Conclusions and Future Work

With the popularization of personal hand-held mobile devices (e.g., smartphones, MP3 players, and PDAs), MSNet is arising recently. Without the constraint of real-time connectivity, MSNet is a more flexible ad hoc network, and has significant impact on future pervasive computing. Being able to improve people's productivity and lives, MSNet has gained high attention from global researchers. Thanks to the hand-held device networking paradigm, the characteristics of MSNet mostly depend on people's mobility. Therefore, the use of Social Network Analysis (SNA) will definitely facilitate the research on MSNet. In this book, we presented the modeling and several application schemes in MSNet.

In Chapter 1, we provided a brief literature review on the development of MSNet and related works. We also explored several realistic datasets to reveal both geographic and social regularities of human mobility, and further proposed the concept of geo-community into MSNet analysis. A semi-Markov process was then employed to model node mobility based on the geo-community structure of the network. Chapter 2 studied the issue of active data broadcasting. The objective was to broadcast data from a supernode to other nodes in the network. The geo-centrality indicating the "dynamic node density" of each geo-community could be derived from the semi-Markov model. Then, several route algorithms were provided considering the geo-centrality information. In Chapter 3, a novel two-hop delegation query (*DelQue*) scheme was presented, which considered query and response integratedly. In contrast to other existing multi-hop search approaches, *DelQue* could lower energy cost dramatically. Furthermore, a spatio-temporal prediction method of node mobility based on semi-Markov model was also proposed to compute neighbors' query utility. Such a lightweight forecasting technique only required nodes to maintain two parameter matrices, making it suitable for a resource-scarce mobile setting. Furthermore, trace-driven simulations showed that the above modeling and application schemes consistently outperformed other existing approaches.

There occurred a close attention on opportunistic mobile network by researchers since it was proposed in 2003. Recently, research achievements increase year by year in the aspect of data acquisition in reality, node mobile model, opportunistic forwarding mechanism and data distribution and retrieval, etc. Worth mentioning that most of the relevant work mainly focused the basic research of the network technology level. However, many supporting technologies are essential to apply MSNet to each field of human society. Some potential critical issues to be solved in MSNets are as follows:

4.1 Energy Efficient Sleep Scheduling for MSNet

In MSNet, data transmission usually relies on hand-held device with Bluetooth function. Bluetooth technology supports short distance, high transmission rate communication between different devices, but under the on-state it can significantly increase the power consumption of the device. Although Bluetooth Special Interest Group (Bluetooth SIG for short) has been committed to the research of the ultra-low power Bluetooth technology. But up to now there hasn't seen any breakthrough. While in opportunistic mobile network, the network is sparse and the connections between nodes aren't frequent, which means the proportion of data transmission time between devices to their Bluetooth opening time is not high. Therefore, form the perspective of energy-saving and cost-reducing, it is very important to research on sleeping scheduling in opportunistic mobile network. General idea can be that predict the future contact time between nodes in the first place, and then wake up the node when it meets a more appropriate one.

In addition, there have been some research achievements in energy efficient sleeping scheduling in traditional wireless sensor network [142], which can be applied to related researches in MSNet.

4.2 Realization of TCP

TCP/IP based on network service model can provide end-to-end communication in different link layer technology. Although not explicitly pointed out, TCP/IP protocol family's steady operation normally relies on the following three assumptions on underlying link characteristics:

1. There exists an end-to-end transmission path between the source node and the destination node.
2. In the network the max Round-Trip Time (RTT for short) between any node pair can't be too long.
3. End-to-end packet loss ratio is small.

However, MSNet violates the above three assumptions. So the traditional TCP/IP protocol family can't provide services for this kind of network. The most challenge thing to realize RRT in opportunistic mobile network is that RRT between nodes in the network is too long. Considering that the nodes which have high contact probability with the destination node have a great opportunity to forward data to the destination node, the initial solution is that we can substitute the relay nodes in this kind for the destination node to return acknowledgement.

4.3 Research on Anycast Service

The initial semantics of anycast is to identify a group of hosts providing specific service through an anycast address in IP network and the service access side does not care about which host provides service (for example DNS or mirroring service). Message accessing to this address can be routed to any host in this group. It provides a stateless and best-effort service.

Anycast service is often used in daily life. For example, if there are backups of data users who want to query in several data center, the user will get the data as long as one data center feedbacks to. Redundant feedbacks result in a waste of resources for the whole network. But now in MSNet, unicast, multicast and broadcast have all been studied, while research on anycast service is still empty. Certainly, transmission with single copy can solve the above problem, but the drawback is long delay; and in the case of multiple copies transmission status is unknown to each other. All of these put forward the challenge to the research on anycast service in MSNets.

4.4 Effective Use of Contact Duration

In existing related studies/research on MSNet, contact duration between nodes is usually assumed to be long enough to transmit all data successfully, or at least transmit one complete data packet successfully. However, in reality, packet size can be big or small and the contact duration time between nodes can be long or short, so we cannot assume the whole data packet can be successfully transmitted during each contact. Therefore, each node needs to determine the order of transmission with the constraint of the size of the data packet to be transmitted so as to utilize each contact efficiently. A general idea is that long contact duration time should be used to transmit large data packets and the cooperation level between pairwise nodes can also be considered.

References

1. K. Fall. A delay-tolerant network architecture for challenged internets. In *Proc. ACM SIGCOMM*, 2003.
2. S. Burleigh, A. Hooke, L. Torgerson, K. Fall, V. Cerf, B. Durst, K. Scott, and H. Weiss. Delay-tolerant networking: an approach to interplanetary internet. *IEEE Communications Magazine*, 41(6):128–136, 2003.
3. A. Mainwaring, D. Culler, J. Polastre, R. Szewczyk, and J. Anderson. Wireless sensor networks for habitat monitoring. In *Proc. ACM WSNA*, pages 88–97, 2002.
4. A. Pentland, R. Fletcher, and A. Hasson. Daknet: Rethinking connectivity in developing nations. *IEEE Computer*, 37(1):78–83, 2004.
5. S. Jain, K. Fall, and R. Patra. Routing in a delay tolerant network. In *Proc. ACM SIGCOMM*, pages 145–158, 2004.
6. M. Musolesi and C. Mascolo. Designing mobility models based on social network theory. *ACM SIGMOBILE Mobile Computing and Communication Review*, 11(3), July 2007.
7. A. Martinez, V. Villarroel, J. Seoane, and F. Del Pozo. Analysis of information and communication needs in rural primary health care in developing countries. *IEEE Trans. on Information Technology in Biomedicine*, 9(1):66–72, 2005.
8. M. Chetty, W. Tucker, and E. Blake. Developing locally relevant software applications for rural areas: a south african example. In *Proc. ACM SAICSIT*, pages 239–243, 2004.
9. L. Lambrinos. Deploying open source ip telephony in rural environments. In *Proc. IEEE NGMAST*, pages 623–627, 2008.
10. B.E. Kolko, E.J. Rose, and E.J. Johnson. Communication as information-seeking: the case for mobile social software for developing regions. In *Proc. ACM WWW*, pages 863–872, 2007.
11. D. Joshi and V. Avasthi. Mobile internet ux for developing countries. In *Proc. MIUE*, 2007.
12. R. Dingledine, N. Mathewson, and P.Syverson. Tor: The second-generation onion router. In *Proc. USENIX-Security*, pages 21–21, 2004.
13. M.K. Reiter and A.D. Rubin. Crowds: Anonymity for web transactions. *ACM Trans. on Information and System Security*, 1(1):66–92, 1998.
14. B. Ahlgren, M. D'Ambrosio, M. Marchisio, I. Marsh, C. Dannewitz, B. Ohlman, K. Pentikousis, O. Strandberg, R. Rembarz, and V. Vercellone. Design considerations for a network of information. In *Proc. ACM CoNEXT*, 2008.
15. P. Hui, A. Lindgren, and J. Crowcroft. Empirical evaluation of hybrid opportunistic networks. In *Proc. IEEE COMSNETS*, 2009.
16. N. Laoutaris, G. Smaragdakis, P. Rodriguez, and R. Sundaram. Delay tolerant bulk data transfers on the internet. In *Proc. ACM SIGMETRICS*, pages 229–238, 2009.
17. P. Hui, R. Mortier, K. Xu, J. Crowcroft, and V.O.K. Li. Sharing airtime with shair avoids wasting time and money. In *Proc. ACM HotMobile*, 2009.

18. A. Chaintreau, P. Hui, J. Crowcroft, C. Diot, R. Gass, and J. Scott. Pocket switched networks: Real-world mobility and its consequences for opportunistic forwarding. *University of Cambridge, Computer Lab, Tech. Rep. UCAM-CL-TR-617, Feb*, 2005.

19. P. Hui, A. Chaintreau, J. Scott, R. Gass, J. Crowcroft, and C. Diot. Pocket switched networks and human mobility in conference environments. In *Proc. ACM SIGCOMM WDNT*, pages 244–251, 2005.

20. M. McNett and G. M. Voelker. Access and mobility of wireless pda users. *ACM SIGMOBILE Mobile Computing and Communications Review*, 9(2):40–55, 2005.

21. T. Henderson, D. Kotz, and I. Abyzov. The changing usage of a mature campus-wide wireless network. In *Proc. ACM MobiCom*, pages 187–201, 2004.

22. D. Kotz and T. Henderson. Crawdad: A community resource for archiving wireless data at dartmouth. *IEEE Pervasive Computing*, pages 12–14, 2005.

23. N. Eagle and A. Pentland. Reality mining: sensing complex social systems. *Personal and Ubiquitous Computing*, 10(4):255–268, 2006.

24. A. Chaintreau, P. Hui, J. Crowcroft, C. Diot, R. Gass, and J. Scott. Impact of human mobility on opportunistic forwarding algorithms. *IEEE Trans. on Mobile Computing*, 6(6):606–620, 2007.

25. J. Krumm and E. Horvitz. The microsoft multiperson location survey. *Microsoft ResearchTechnical Report*, 2005.

26. T. Camp, J. Boleng, and V. Davies. A survey of mobility models for ad hoc network research. *Wireless Communications and Mobile Computing (WCMC)*, 2(5):483–502, 2002.

27. A. Einstein. *Investigations on the Theory of the Brownian Movement*. 1956.

28. K. Hermann. Modeling the sociological aspect of mobility in ad hoc networks. In *Proc. ACM MSWiM*, pages 128–129, 2003.

29. D. B. Johnson and D. A. Maltz. Dynamic source routing in ad hoc wireless networks. *Mobile Computing*, pages 153–181, 1996.

30. J. Y. Le Boudec and M. Vojnovic. Perfect simulation and stationarity of a class of mobility models. In *Proc. IEEE INFOCOM*, pages 2743–2754, 2005.

31. J. Y. Le Boudec and M. Vojnovic. The random trip model: stability, stationary regime, and perfect simulation. *IEEE/ACM Trans. on Networking*, 14(6):1153–1166, 2006.

32. J. Y. Le Boudec. Understanding the simulation of mobility models with palm calculus. *Performance Evaluation*, 64(2):126–147, 2007.

33. W. Navidi and T. Camp. Stationary distributions for the random waypoint mobility model. *IEEE Trans. on Mobile Computing*, 3(1):99–108, 2004.

34. D. Tang and M. Baker. Analysis of a local-area wireless network. In *Proc. ACM MobiCom*, pages 1–10, 2000.

35. A. Balachandran, G. M. Voelker, P. Bahl, and P. V. Rangan. Characterizing user behavior and network performance in a public wireless lan. In *Proc. ACM SIGMETRICS*, volume 30, pages 195–205, 2002.

36. M. Balazinska and P. Castro. Characterizing mobility and network usage in a corporate wireless local-area network. In *Proc. ACM MobiSys*, pages 303–316, 2003.

37. C. Tuduce and T. Gross. A mobility model based on wlan traces and its validation. In *Proc. IEEE INFOCOM*, pages 664–674, 2005.

38. D. Bhattacharjee, A. Rao, C. Shah, M. Shah, and A. Helmy. Empirical modeling of campus-wide pedestrian mobility observations on the usc campus. In *Proc. IEEE VTC-Fall*, pages 2887–2891, 2004.

39. W. Hsu, K. Merchant, H. Shu, C. Hsu, and A. Helmy. Weighted waypoint mobility model and its impact on ad hoc networks. *ACM Mobile Computer Communications Review (MC2R)*, 9(1):59–63, 2005.

40. R. Jain, D. Lelescu, and M. Balakrishnan. Model t: an empirical model for user registration patterns in a campus wireless lan. In *Proc. ACM MobiCom*, pages 170–184, 2005.

41. D. Lelescu, U. C. Kozat, R. Jain, and M. Balakrishnan. Model t++: an empirical joint space-time registration model. In *Proc. ACM MobiHoc*, pages 61–72, 2006.

42. J. Yoon, B. D. Noble, M. Liu, and M. Kim. Building realistic mobility models from coarse-grained traces. In *Proc. ACM MobiSys*, pages 177–190, 2006.

43. M. Kim, D. Kotz, and S. Kim. Extracting a mobility model from real user traces. In *Proc. IEEE INFOCOM*, 2006.

44. G. Resta and P. Santi. The qos-rwp mobility and user behavior model for public area wireless networks. In *Proc. ACM MSWiM*, pages 375–384, 2006.

45. K. Maeda, K. Sato, K. Konishi, A. Yamasaki, A. Uchiyama, H. Yamaguchi, K. Yasumoto, and T. Higashino. Getting urban pedestrian flow from simple observation: Realistic mobility generation in wireless network simulation. In *Proc. ACM MSWiM*, pages 151–158, 2005.

46. A. K. Saha and D. B. Johnson. Modeling mobility for vehicular ad-hoc networks. In *Proc. ACM VANET*, pages 91–92, 2004.

47. R. Mangharam, D. S. Weller, D. D. Stancil, R. Rajkumar, and J. S. Parikh. Groovesim: a topography-accurate simulator for geographic routing in vehicular networks. In *Proc. ACM VANET*, pages 59–68, 2005.

48. D. R. Choffnes and F. E. Bustamante. An integrated mobility and traffic model for vehicular wireless networks. In *Proc. ACM VANET*, pages 69–78, 2005.

49. X. Zhang, J. Kurose, B. N. Levine, D. Towsley, and H. Zhang. Study of a bus-based disruption-tolerant network: mobility modeling and impact on routing. In *Proc. ACM Mobi-Com*, pages 195–206, 2007.

50. E.M. Daly and M. Haahr. Social network analysis for routing in disconnected delay-tolerant manets. In *Proc. ACM MobiHoc*, pages 32–40, 2007.

51. P. Costa, C. Mascolo, M. Musolesi, and G.P. Picco. Socially-aware routing for publish-subscribe in delay-tolerant mobile ad hoc networks. *IEEE Journal on Selected Areas in Communications (JSAC)*, 26(5):748–760, 2008.

52. M. Musolesi and C. Mascolo. A community based mobility model for ad hoc network research. In *Proc. ACM SIGMOBILE REALMAN*, pages 31–38, 2006.

53. D. J. Watts. *Small worlds: the dynamics of networks between order and randomness*. 2003.

54. I. Glauche, W. Krause, R. Sollacher, and M. Greiner. Continuum percolation of wireless ad hoc communication networks. *Physica A*, 325(3-4):577–600, 2003.

55. T. Spyropoulos, K. Psounis, and C.S. Raghavendra. Performance analysis of mobility-assisted routing. In *Proc. ACM MobiHoc*, pages 49–60, 2006.

56. W. Hsu, T. Spyropoulos, K. Psounis, and A. Helmy. Modeling time-variant user mobility in wireless mobile networks. In *Proc. IEEE INFOCOM*, pages 758–766, 2007.

57. F. Ekman, A. Keränen, J. Karvo, and J. Ott. Working day movement model. In *Proc. ACM MobilityModels*, pages 33–40, 2008.

58. J. Broch, D. A. Maltz, D. B. Johnson, Y. C. Hu, and J. Jetcheva. A performance comparison of multi-hop wireless ad hoc network routing protocols. In *Proc. ACM MobiCom*, pages 85–97, 1998.

59. J. Su, A. Chin, A. Popivanova, A. Goel, and E. de Lara. User mobility for opportunistic ad-hoc networking. In *Proc. IEEE WMCSA*, pages 41–50, 2004.

60. A. Miklas, K. Gollu, K. Chan, S. Saroiu, K. Gummadi, and E. De Lara. Exploiting social interactions in mobile systems. In *Proc. ACM UbiComp*, pages 409–428, 2007.

61. E. Yoneki, P. Hui, and J. Crowcroft. Visualizing community detection in opportunistic networks. In *Proc. ACM CHANTS*, pages 93–96, 2007.

62. V. Srinivasan, M. Motani, and W.T. Ooi. Analysis and implications of student contact patterns derived from campus schedules. In *Proc. ACM MobiCom*, pages 86–97, 2006.

63. C. Boldrini, M. Conti, and A. Passarella. Impact of social mobility on routing protocols for opportunistic networks. In *Proc. IEEE WoWMoM*, 2007.

64. C. Boldrini, M. Conti, J. Jacopini, and A. Passarella. Hibop: a history based routing protocol for opportunistic networks. In *Proc. IEEE WoWMoM*, 2007.

65. P. Hui, J. Crowcroft, and E. Yoneki. Bubble rap: Social-based forwarding in delay tolerant networks. In *Proc. ACM MobiHoc*, 2008.

66. C. Boldrini, M. Conti, and A. Passarella. Modelling data dissemination in opportunistic networks. In *Proc. ACM CHANTS*, pages 89–96, 2008.

67. E. Yoneki, P. Hui, S.Y. Chan, and J. Crowcroft. A socio-aware overlay for publish/subscribe communication in delay tolerant networks. In *Proc. ACM MSWiM*, pages 225–234, 2007.

68. C. Boldrini, M. Conti, and A. Passarella. Contentplace: social-aware data dissemination in opportunistic networks. In *Proc. ACM MSWiM*, pages 203–210, 2008.

69. S. Ioannidis, A. Chaintreau, and L. Massoulié. Optimal and scalable distribution of content updates over a mobile social network. In *Proc. IEEE INFOCOM*, pages 1422–1430, 2009.

70. M. Motani, V. Srinivasan, and P. S. Nuggehalli. PeopleNet: engineering a wireless virtual social network. In *Proc. ACM MobiCom*.

71. J. Ghosh, S. J. Philip, and C. Qiao. Sociological orbit aware location approximation and routing (SOLAR) in MANET. *Ad Hoc Networks*, 5(2):189–209, 2007.

72. W. Gao, Q. Li, B. Zhao, and G. Cao. Multicasting in delay tolerant networks: A social network perspective. In *Proc. ACM MobiHoc*, 2009.

73. F. Bai and A. Helmy. Impact of mobility on last encounter routing protocols. In *Proc. IEEE SECON*, pages 461–470, 2007.

74. W. Gao and G. Cao. On exploiting transient contact patterns for data forwarding in delay tolerant networks. In *Proc. IEEE ICNP*, 2010.

75. Q. Li, S. Zhu, and G. Cao. Routing in socially selfish delay tolerant networks. In *Proc. IEEE INFOCOM*, 2010.

76. Y. Zhang, J. Zhao, G. Cao, and C. Das. On interest locality in content-based routing for largescale manets. In *Proc. IEEE MASS*, pages 178–187, 2009.

77. T. Karagiannis, J. Boudec, and M. Vojnovic. Power law and exponential decay of inter contact times between mobile devices. In *Proc. ACM MobiCom*, 2007.

78. Y. Wang, B. Krishnamachari, and T. W. Valente. Findings from an empirical study of fine-grained human social contacts. In *Proc. IEEE WONS*, pages 153–160, 2009.

79. W. Hsu, D. Dutta, and A. Helmy. Mining behavioral groups in large wireless lans. In *Proc. ACM MobiCom*, pages 338–341, 2007.

80. J. Zhao and G. Cao. VADD: vehicle-assisted data delivery in vehicular ad hoc networks. *IEEE Trans. on Vehicular Technology*, 57(3):1910–1922, May 2008.

81. Y. Zhang, J. Zhao, and G. Cao. Roadcast: a popularity aware content sharing scheme in vanets. *ACM SIGMOBILE Mobile Computing and Communications Review*, 13(4):1–14, 2010.

82. S. Kapadia, B. Krishnamachari, and S. Ghandeharizadeh. Static replication strategies for content availability in vehicular ad-hoc networks. *Mobile Networks and Applications*, 14(5):590–610, 2009.

83. S. Ghandeharizadeh and S. Kapadia. An evaluation of location-demographic replacement policies for zebroids. In *Proc. IEEE CCNC*, 2006.

84. T. Small and Z. J. Haas. The shared wireless infostation model: a new ad hoc networking paradigm (or where there is a whale, there is a way). In *Proc. ACM MobiHoc*, pages 233–244, 2003.

85. X. Zhang, G. Neglia, J. Kurose, and D. Towsley. Performance modeling of epidemic routing. *Computer Networks*, 51(10):827–839, 2006.

86. B. Han, P. Hui, V. S. A. Kumar, M. V. Marathe, and G. Pei. Cellular traffic offloading through opportunistic communications: A case study. In *Proc. ACM CHANTS*, 2010.

87. J. Wu and F. Dai. Efficient broadcasting with guaranteed coverage in mobile ad hoc networks. *IEEE Trans. on Mobile Computing*, 4(3):259–270, May/June 2005.

88. S. Yang and J. Wu. Efficient broadcasting using network coding and directional antennas in MANETs. *IEEE Trans. on Parallel and Distributed Systems*, 21(2):148–161, Feb. 2010.

89. A. Vahdat and D. Becker. Epidemic routing for partially connected ad hoc networks. (CS-200006), 2000.

90. F. J. Ros, P. M. Ruiz, and I. Stojmenovic. Acknowledgment-based broadcast protocol for reliable and efficient data dissemination in vehicular ad-hoc networks. *IEEE Trans. on Mobile Computing*, 11(1):33–46, Jan 2012.

91. W. Zhao, M. Ammar, and E. Zegura. A message ferrying approach for data delivery in sparse mobile ad hoc networks. In *Proc. ACM MobiHoc*, 2004.

92. W. Zhao, M. Ammar, and E. Zegura. Controlling the mobility of multiple data transport ferries in a delay-tolerant network. In *Proc. IEEE INFOCOM*, 2005.

93. R. Shah, S. Roy, S. Jain, and W. Brunette. Data MULEs: Modeling a three-tier architecture for sparse sensor networks. *Ad Hoc Networks*, 1:215–233, Sep. 2003.
94. J. Wu, S. Yang, and F. Dai. Logarithmic store-carry-forward routing in mobile ad hoc networks. *IEEE Trans. on Parallel and Distributed Systems*, 18(6):735–748, Jun. 2007.
95. M. Tariq, M. Ammar, and E. Zegura. Message ferry route design for sparse ad hoc networks with mobile nodes. In *Proc. ACM MobiHoc*, 2006.
96. S. Milgram. The small world problem. *Psychology Today*, 2(1):60–67, 1967.
97. Q. Yuan, I. Cardei, and J. Wu. Predict and relay: An efficient routing in disruption-tolerant networks. In *Proc. ACM MobiHoc*, 2009.
98. N. Sarafijanovic-Djukic, M. Pidrkowski, and M. Grossglauser. Island hopping: Efficient mobility-assisted forwarding in partitioned networks. In *Proc. IEEE SECON*, 2006.
99. J. Scott, R. Gass, J. Crowcroft, P. Hui, C. Diot, and A. Chaintreau. CRAWDAD data set cambridge/haggle (v. 2009-05-29). Downloaded from http://crawdad.cs.dartmouth.edu/cambridge/haggle, May 2009.
100. N. Eagle, A. Pentland, and D. Lazer. Inferring social network structure using mobile phone data. In *Proc. PNAS*, volume 106(36), pages 15274–15278, 2009.
101. A. Peddemors, H. Eertink, and I. Niemegeers. CoSphere data set. Downloaded from http://crawdad.cs.dartmouth.edu/novay/cosphere, May 2008.
102. P. Hui, E. Yoneki, S. Chan, and J. Crowcroft. Distributed community detection in delay tolerant networks. In *Proc. ACM MobiArch*, 2007.
103. J. Lee and J. Hou. Modeling steady-state and transient behaviors of user mobility: Formulation, analysis, and application. In *Proc. ACM MobiHoc*, 2006.
104. S. Boyd and L. Vandenberghe. Convex optimization. *Cambridge University Press*, 2004.
105. W. Cook, D. Applegate, R. Bixby, and V. Chvatal. Concorde: A code for solution of travelling salesman problem. http://www.tsp.gatech.edu/.
106. V. Vazirani. Approximation algorithms. *Springer*, Aug. 2001.
107. H. Kellerer, U. Pferschy, and D. Pisinger. *Kanpsack Problems*. Springer, Berlin, 2004.
108. J. Fan, Y. Du, W. Gao, J. Chen, and Y. Sun. Geography-aware active data dissemination in mobile social networks. In *Proc. IEEE MASS*, 2010.
109. R. Jain, A. Durresi, and G. Babicl. Throughput fairness index: An explanation. http://www.cse.wustl.edu/jain/atmf/a99-0045.htm, Feb. 1999.
110. L. D. Bodin, B. L. Golden, A. A. Assad, and M. Ball. Routing and scheduling of vehicles and crews: The state of the arts. *Computers and Operations Research*, 10(2):63–212, 1983.
111. V. Maniezzo, R. Baldacci, M. Boschetti, and M. Zamboni. Scatter search methods for the covering tour problem. *Metaheuristic Optimization via Memory and Evolution: Tabu Search and Scatter Search*, 30:59–91, 2005.
112. U. Shevade, H. Song, L. Qiu, , and Y. Zhang. Incentive-aware routing in DTNs. In *Proc. IEEE ICNP*, 2008.
113. B. Chen and M. Chan. MobiCent: a credit-based incentive system for disruption tolerant network. In *Proc. IEEE INFOCOM*, 2010.
114. T. Spyropoulos, K. Psounis, and C. Raghavendra. Spray and wait: An efficient routing scheme for intermittently connected mobile networks. In *Proc. ACM SIGCOMM*, 2005.
115. T. Spyropoulos, K. Psounis, and C. Raghavendra. Spray and focus: Efficient mobility-assisted routing for heterogeneous and correlated mobility. In *Proc. IEEE PerCom*, 2007.
116. J. Burgess, B. Gallagher, D. Jensen, and B. Levine. Maxprop: Routing for vehicle-based disruption-tolerant networks. In *Proc. IEEE INFOCOM*, 2006.
117. V. Erramilli, A. Chaintreau, M. Crovella, and C. Diot. Delegation forwarding. In *Proc. ACM MobiHoc*, 2008.
118. A. Balasubramanian, B. Levine, and A. Lindgren. DTN routing as a resource allocation problem. In *Proc. ACM SIGCOMM*, 2007.
119. S. He, J. Chen, Y. Sun, D. K. Y. Yau, and N. K. Yip. On optimal information capture by energy-constrained mobile sensors. *IEEE Trans. on Vehicular Technology*, 59(5), Jun. 2010.
120. H. Zhu, X. Lin, R. Lu, Y. Fan, and X. Shen. SMART: A secure multilayer credit-based incentive scheme for delay-tolerant networks. *IEEE Trans. on Vehicular Technology*, 58(8):4628–4639, Oct. 2009.

121. D. Niyato and P. Wang. Optimization of the mobile router and traffic sources in vehicular delay tolerant network. *IEEE Trans. on Vehicular Technology*, 58(9):5095–5104, Nov. 2009.

122. X. Zhang, H. Zhang, and Y. Gu. Impact of source counter on dtn routing control under resource constraints. In *Proc. ACM MobiOpp*, 2010.

123. C. Singh, A. Kumar, and R. Sundaresan. Delay and energy optimal two-hop relaying in delay tolerant networks. In *Proc. IEEE WiOpt*, 2010.

124. G. Neglia and X. Zhang. Optimal delay-power trade-off in sparse delay tolerant networks: a preliminary study. In *SIGCOMM Challenged Network workshop*, 2006.

125. T. Spyropoulos, K. Psounis, and C. Raghavendra. Efficient routing in intermittently connected mobile networks: The multiple-copy case. *IEEE/ACM Trans. on Networking*, 16(1):77–90, 2008.

126. V. Lenders, G. Karlsson, and M. May. Wireless ad hoc podcasting. In *Proc. IEEE SECON*, 2007.

127. M. Piorkowski, N. Sarafijanovic-Djukic, and M. Grossglauser. CRAWDAD data set epfl/mobility (v. 2009-02-24). Downloaded from http://crawdad.cs.dartmouth.edu/epfl/mobility, 2009.

128. Y. Du, J. Fan, and J. Chen. Experimental analysis of user mobility pattern in mobile social networks. In *Proc. IEEE WCNC*, 2011.

129. G. Corradi, J. Janssen, and R. Manca. Numerical treatment of homogeneous semi-markov processes in transient case - a straightforward approach. *Methodology and Computing in Applied Probability*, 6:233–246, 2004.

130. N. B. Chang and M. Liu. Controlled flooding search in a large network. *IEEE/ACM Trans. on Networking*, 15(2):436–449, 2007.

131. C. Avin and C. Brito. Efficient and robust query processing in dynamic environments using random walk techniques. In *Proc. IEEE/ACM IPSN*, 2004.

132. S. D. Servetto and G. Barrenechea. Constrained random walks on random graphs: routing algorithms for large scale wireless sensor networks. In *Proc. ACM WSNA*, 2002.

133. T. Hara. Effective replica allocation in ad hoc networks for improving data accessibility. In *Proc. IEEE INFOCOM*, 2001.

134. M. Stillerman. Hot Diffusion: peer to peer tactical information management platform. In *DARPA DTN Phase II Kickoff meeting*, 2006.

135. W. W. Terpstra, J. Kangasharju, C. Leng, and A. P. Buchmann. BubbleStorm: resilient, probabilistic, and exhaustive peer-to-peer search. In *Proc. ACM SIGCOMM*, 2007.

136. B. Yang and A. R. Hurson. Content-aware search of multimedia data in ad hoc networks. In *Proc. ACM MSWiM*, 2005.

137. A. Balasubramanian, Y. Zhou, W. B. Croft, B. N. Levine, and A. Venkataramani. Web search from a bus. In *Proc. ACM CHANTS*, 2007.

138. J. Ott and M. J. Pitkanen. DTN-based content storage and retrieval. In *Proc. ACM AOC*, 2007.

139. P. Hui, J. Leguay, J. Crowcroft, J. Scott, T. Friedman, and V. Conan. Osmosis in pocket switched networks. In *Proc. ChinaCom*, 2006.

140. L. A. Adamic, B. A. Huberman, R. M. Lukose, and A. R. Puniyani. Search in power-law networks. *Physical Review E*, 64(4):046135, Sep. 2001.

141. M. J. Pitkanen and J. Ott. Redundancy and distributed caching in mobile DTNs. In *Proc. ACM MobiArch*, 2007.

142. Y. Gu and T. He. Data forwarding in extremely low duty-cycle sensor networks with unreliable communication links. In *Proc. ACM SenSys*, pages 321–334, 2007.